FOUNDATIONS OF MODERN PSYCHOLOGY SERIES

Richard S. Lazarus, Editor

SARNOFF A. MEDNICK

Professor of Psychology
New School of Social Research

HOWARD R. POLLIO

Professor of Psychology
University of Tennessee

ELIZABETH F. LOFTUS

Professor of Psychology
New School of Social Research

second edition

Learning

PRENTICE-HALL, INC., ENGLEWOOD CLIFFS, NEW JERSEY

Library of Congress Cataloging in Publication Data

MEDNICK, SARNOFF A
   Learning.

   1. Learning, Psychology of. I. Pollio, Howard R.,
joint author. II. Loftus, Elizabeth F.,
joint author. III. Title.
LB1051.M435 1973   153.1'5   73–4796
ISBN 0–13–527127–4
ISBN 0–13–527101–0 (pbk.)

© 1973, 1964 by

Prentice-Hall, Inc., Englewood Cliffs, N.J.

10   9   8   7   6   5   4   3   2   1

Prentice-Hall International, Inc., London

Prentice-Hall of Australia, Pty. Ltd., Sydney

Prentice-Hall of Canada, Ltd., Toronto

Prentice-Hall of India Private Limited, New Delhi

Prentice-Hall of Japan, Inc., Tokyo

Contents

THREE

Simple Learning

CLASSICAL AND OPERANT CONDITIONING *23*

CLASSICAL CONDITIONING

SIMPLE LEARNING: A SUMMARY AND COMPARISON

FOUR

Complex Habits

THE LEARNING OF SERIAL RESPONSE PATTERNS *53*

FIVE

Motivation and Learning *67*

THE MEASUREMENT OF MOTIVATION

TYPES OF MOTIVES

DOES MOTIVATION AFFECT LEARNING OR PERFORMANCE?

SIX

The Learning of Concepts and the Transfer of Learning *87*

SEVEN

Remembering and Forgetting *103*

MEASURING MEMORY

FORGETTING: FIVE EXPLANATIONS

SHORT-TERM AND LONG-TERM MEMORY

EIGHT

Foundations of
Modern Psychology Series

The tremendous growth and vitality of psychology and its increasing fusion with the social and biological sciences demand a search for new approaches to teaching at the introductory level. We can no longer feel content with the traditional basic course, geared as it usually is to a single text that tries to skim everything, that sacrifices depth for breadth. Psychology has become too diverse for any one person, or group, to write about with complete authority. The alternative, a book that ignores many essential areas in order to present more comprehensively and effectively a particular aspect or view of psychology, is also insufficient, for in this solution many key areas are simply not communicated to the student at all.

The Foundations of Modern Psychology Series was the first in what has become a growing trend in psychology toward groups of short texts dealing with various basic subjects, each written by an active authority. It was conceived with the idea of providing greater flexibility for instructors teaching general courses than was ordinarily available in the large, encyclopedic textbooks, and greater depth of presentation for individual topics not typically given much space in introductory textbooks.

The earliest volumes appeared in 1963, the latest not until 1973. Well over one and a quarter million copies, collectively, have been sold, attesting to the widespread use of these books in the teaching of psychology. Individual volumes have been used as supplementary texts, or as *the* text, in various undergraduate courses in psychology, education, public health, and sociology, and clusters of volumes have served as the text in beginning undergraduate courses in general psychology. Groups of volumes have been translated into eight languages, including Dutch, Hebrew, Italian, Japanese, Polish, Portuguese, Spanish, and Swedish.

With wide variation in publication date and type of content, some of the volumes need revision, while others do not. We have left this decision to the individual author who best knows his book in relation to the state of the field. Some will remain unchanged, some will be modestly changed, and still others completely rewritten. In the new series edition, we have also opted for some variation in the length and style of individual books, to reflect the different ways in which they have been used as texts.

There has never been stronger interest in good teaching in our colleges and universities than there is now; and for this the availability of high quality, well-written, and stimulating text materials highlighting the exciting and continuing search for knowledge is a prime prerequisite. This is especially the case in undergraduate courses where large numbers of students must have access to suitable readings. The Foundations of Modern Psychology Series represents our ongoing attempt to provide college teachers with the best textbook materials we can create.

Richard S. Lazarus, Editor

Preface

A preface should be brief, all the more so if it introduces a second edition. Perhaps it will suffice to indicate that this edition attempts to reflect advances in the field of learning in the nine years since the first edition.

For this reason the second half of the book has undergone the most extensive alterations. Chapter Eight is completely new, and deals with disturbances in human memory and the practical implication of memory principles for studying and remembering. This represents a substantial shift from our first edition where the preface stated "applications are not mentioned . . . in this book." Attention to applications may also be found in other sections of this volume (e.g., discussion of therapy for psychological disturbances using principles of operant conditioning). But this shift reflects current movements in the field toward the practical utilization of learning principles in education, mental health, and industry. All in all, our intention in this edition, as in the previous one, is to interest the undergraduate student in the study of learning, certainly one of the key topics in contemporary psychology.

Acknowledgments

Mednick wishes to especially thank Dr. Robert Leeper for his kindness in permitting us to have the benefit of his margin notes on the first edition. It has enabled us to eliminate many unclear statements and inaccuracies. Mednick spent a year with Dr. Leeper at the University of Oregon and owes much to the influence of his approach to the understanding of learning phenomena.

Joyce Nathan, Sif Wiksten, William Cole, and Ann Bailey were of great help in the preparation of this edition.

Some Examples of
Research on Learning

chapter one

The planarian is a very simple, cross-eyed flatworm that lives on the underside of rocks in mildly stagnant, polluted water. In many ways, the planarian, only three-quarters of an inch long, is an interesting creature—mainly because, tiny and uncomplex as it is, it can learn (see Figure 1–1).

The first experiments using planaria were performed by James V. McConnell and his associates, who used electroshocks to teach them to cringe whenever a hundred-watt light bulb a few inches from their heads was turned on. We can assume that the flatworm's response to the light stimulus was *learned*—as opposed to *reflexive*—because when the lamp was first turned on, for a three-second flash, it took little notice of the light. But during training, in the last of the three seconds that the light remained on, the planarian was regularly jolted with an electric shock delivered through the water. The planarian did not have to learn its response to the shock; it is a reflexive body contraction. If the light and shock were presented together about 250 times, the contraction response was regularly produced by the light that had previously been ignored. Now, given the light flash, the response of body contractions was a foregone conclusion.

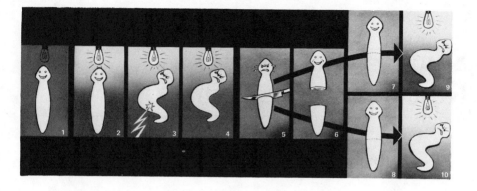

FIGURE 1–1.   In terms of evolution, planaria are the earliest organisms to have
developed a concentration of nerve fibers that could be called a "brain." Because
of this, researchers have been interested in the planarian's ability to learn. The
first four panels of this figure are discussed in the text. When a light and electric
shock are paired, as in panel 3, planaria eventually learn to respond to the light
with contraction, the response they ordinarily give to the shock (as in panel 4).
If a planarian is cut into pieces, each piece regenerates a complete organism.
James V. McConnell, Allan L. Jacobson, and Daniel P. Kimble took planaria
which had learned to contract to the light and cut them in half (panels 5 and 6).
They then allowed the halves to regenerate as in panels 7 and 8. The question
was: if each half was then tested with the light would any memory be shown?
Would the head end show better memory than the tail end? As is illustrated in
panels 9 and 10, both heads and tails showed retention of the light-contraction
association. Of special interest is the fact that there was no difference in the
amount of retention exhibited in the head and tail ends. The intriguing question
stemming from this research is: How does retention occur in the tail section?
Recent evidence suggests that it is partially chemical in nature.

   McConnell also reported that when well-trained worms were chopped
up and fed to untrained worms, the latter learned to cringe in response
to a light stimulus much more rapidly than planarians whose diets did
not include previously trained worms. From these early experiments, it
appeared as if some chemical change in the original animal brought
about by his learning experience could be transmitted to another animal,
and that this second animal would then show similar behavior. On this
basis, it looked as if there were some powerful transmitting substance
that could be transferred from one organism to another.
   Several psychologists have used these and other results to support the
notion that a specific chemical molecule (the RNA molecule) is somehow involved in learning and the structure of memory. At the present
time, however, it seems more reasonable to agree with Stanford University's brain researcher Karl H. Pribram, who has pointed out that trying
to understand learning and memory by studying the physiology of the

brain is like "looking for the difference between jazz and symphonic music by studying the bumps on a record." In other words, although the material structure of a record (the "bumps") in contact with the needle produces the music we hear, nevertheless the music is not the bumps, nor are the bumps the music. The configuration of the bumps simply determines that the electrical impulses will faithfully play back the music that was recorded.

For our purposes, then, the most important thing to note about the planarian experiments is that, despite the fact that the planarian is a very simple organism, *it can learn*—and that such learning can be, and has been, regularly demonstrated in the laboratory.

Some Basics of Learning

CLASSICAL CONDITIONING

The method used to train the planarian is called *classical conditioning*. It consists of repeatedly pairing a neutral stimulus (in this case, a light) with another stimulus that invariably elicits a response (in this case, an electric shock producing a contraction) until finally the neutral stimulus alone elicits the same response. Such conditioning was first systematically investigated by the Russian physiologist Ivan Pavlov. Pavlov's basic method involved performing an operation on the cheek of a dog so that part of the dog's salivary gland was exposed. A recording device was attached to the dog that measured the flow of saliva. The dog was then brought to the laboratory and the classical conditioning procedure begun. First, a light (the conditioned stimulus—which is at first neutral) was turned on. The dog did not salivate. Less than one second later some meat powder (the unconditioned stimulus) was given to the dog. The dog began to eat and the recording device indicated that the dog was salivating quite a bit. The whole procedure was repeated: light–meat powder–salivation and eating. After several repetitions of this procedure, the dog began to salivate as soon as the light was turned on and continued to do so even though the meat powder was no longer given to him (see Figure 1–2.).

There is a great deal of similarity between the classical conditioning of planaria and Pavlov's experiment with dogs. In both cases, an association was formed—between a neutral stimulus and a response— through the pairing of the neutral stimulus (conditioned stimulus) with an unconditioned stimulus that invariably elicits the response. In later chapters we shall consider classical conditioning in greater detail, for

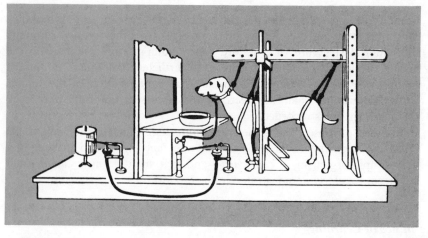

FIGURE 1–2. Pavlov's experimental arrangement. (From D. J. Lewis, *Scientific principles of psychology*, Englewood Cliffs, N.J.: Prentice-Hall, 1963.)

despite its apparent simplicity classical conditioning is not a single phenomenon and seems to have wide implications for complicated human and animal behavior.

OPERANT CONDITIONING

When you teach a dog to sit or to roll over, or a child to tapdance or ride a bike, you may be using *operant conditioning* procedures. What you usually do in these cases is to induce the dog or child to do what you want him to, afterwards rewarding him with either a doggie bone, a piece of candy, or approval. This type of conditioning procedure was first systematically studied and reported by B. F. Skinner in 1938. Although Skinner did most of his original work with white rats as laboratory subjects, his methods have found broad application.

To get a better idea of what such conditioning is all about, consider this story concerning a project being conducted in a Massachusetts mental hospital, where experiments are carried on in specially constructed rooms that happen to be in the basement of the building. Dealing with very seriously disturbed patients, the experimenters often found it quite difficult to get the patients to come down to the experiment rooms. An undergraduate from a nearby university, well versed in operant conditioning procedures, took it upon himself to try to bring a patient with a long-standing mental illness to one of these rooms. Illness had reduced this patient to a near-animal state; his speech had become increasingly unintelligible and his motor control was beginning to deteriorate. He had little or no control over defecation and urination and would often bite individuals who came too close to him. Consequently, he was kept in virtual isolation.

In order to get him downstairs, the student used an operant conditioning technique called "shaping." In this method the experimenter continually rewards acts that come closer and closer to the behavior ultimately desired. Thus, the student waited for the first time the patient turned his head toward the door leading to the basement stairs. At this point he presented the patient with a small piece of candy, which the latter quickly ate (it had been previously determined that the patient liked candy). Soon the patient faced the door again, and again the student rewarded this behavior with a piece of candy. After a number of such incidents the patient then stood facing the door: the candy had acted as a reward for door-facing and had increased the likelihood, or probability, of its occurrence. After this phase of training was completed, the student withheld candy until the patient took a step. When the patient had received the candy several times for taking steps, the student again withheld candy until the patient took steps in the direction of the basement stairs. After a number of days, during which there were many reversals and disappointments, the patient actually walked down the stairs, entered a basement room, and went through the experimental procedures, the first time in some years that this patient had behaved in such an organized manner.

This example of shaping illustrates the effectiveness of systematically administered reward, the most important feature of operant conditioning. Shaping has also been applied to education by teachers and teaching machines. A teacher cannot sit back and wait for a student to solve a mathematical word problem before reinforcing the student. When developing such a complex performance, the teacher or teaching machine will first reinforce the behavior of solving simple addition and subtraction problems. After this phase of training, reward is withheld until the student solves more complex arithmetic problems. When a student has been rewarded several times for complex problems, he is presented with a simple arithmetic word problem such as: "A bushel of corn weighs 6 lb; how much will 2 bushels weigh?" Proceeding in this fashion, we find that after a period of time the student will be able to solve more complicated mathematical work problems such as: "Every day the Greasy Spoon Restaurant makes 37 poached eggs, 46 fried eggs, 15 cheese omelettes with 3 eggs in each omelette, and 43 scrambled eggs. If 57 people eat in the Greasy Spoon, and each person eats the same number of eggs, how many eggs does each person eat?" Essentially, the student is rewarded for progressing in small stages toward acquiring the desired information or skills.

Operant conditioning differs from classical conditioning in certain ways. Most importantly, classical conditioning only applies in situations where a response is inevitable. In the planarian, for instance, contraction is an automatic reflex to electric shock; in Pavlov's dogs, salivation is an automatic response to the presentation of meat powder. In operant conditioning, the experimenter must patiently wait for some response to occur naturally before he can increase its probability with a reward. We shall discuss this and other differences and their implications in Chapter 3.

MAZE LEARNING

We can analyze both classical and operant conditioning in terms of *stimuli, responses,* and *rewards.* In order to study these units as they combine in complex series, psychologists have devised a number of different procedures. Among these the maze has been one of the most

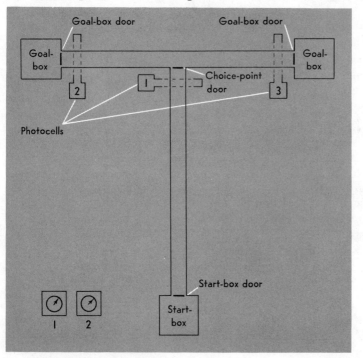

FIGURE 1–3. Drawing of a simple T-maze. Rat is placed in the starting box, and when he is facing forward, the door is raised. The door is closed to prevent him from retracing his steps. When the animal crosses photocell 1, the first clock is stopped, giving a measure of running time from the opening of the start-box door to reaching the choice point. When the animal reaches either photocell 2 or 3, clock 2 is stopped, giving a measure of the total time from opening the start-box door to reaching one of the goal boxes. Once the rat enters the goal box the door is dropped to detain him there until he consumes the reward. (From D. J. Lewis, *Scientific principles of psychology,* Englewood Cliffs, N.J.: Prentice-Hall, 1963.)

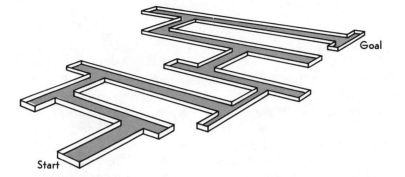

FIGURE 1-4. A schematic representation of a multiple T-maze. The door here shown is at the entrance; interior doors are not shown.

widely used with animals. The simplest form is the *T-maze* (Figure 1–3) where an animal must choose between a left or right turn at the point of choice. If he chooses correctly he is rewarded with food in the goal box. The setup may be further complicated by adding more points of choice, as in the multiple T-maze (Figure 1–4).

VERBAL LEARNING

Besides mazes, psychologists also use various forms of verbal tasks to study learning processes. In one method, called *serial verbal learning*, subjects are asked to learn to recite a series of words in order to find out something about how people go about learning sequential tasks. One of the pioneers in verbal learning research, Hermann Ebbinghaus, wanted to study verbal learning without the troublesome contaminating effects of the previous experience people have with words. To get around this problem he utilized verbal units that subjects could not have previously experienced—*nonsense syllables*, relatively meaningless three-letter combinations composed of a vowel flanked by two consonants—for example, *xad*. Ebbinghaus's strategy was only partially successful, however, for it was soon discovered that even nonsense syllables are affected by previous experience. For example, *syn* is close enough to a familiar English word to act in learning experiments in almost the same way as does the real three-letter word. This property of nonsense syllables is called their *meaningfulness*, and lists of nonsense syllables have been rated for their degree of meaningfulness by determining how regularly these syllables tend to suggest associated words or ideas to groups of judges. Research has shown, for example, that lists of nonsense syllables that are relatively higher in meaningfulness are learned more quickly.

Learning and Higher Mental Processes

Up to this point, we have been concerned with relatively low-level instances of learning. In this section we shall try to correct this unbalanced picture. Perhaps this can be done most appropriately by describing some of the research of a man whose work was aimed at correcting this imbalance for the field of psychology as a whole.

On an island off the coast of Africa, Wolfgang Köhler performed a series of experiments that were designed to challenge certain simplistic explanations in psychology. Detained on this island by the Allies during World War I, Köhler took this opportunity to conduct a study that formed the basis of his book *The Mentality of Apes*. Köhler undertook this work partly in an attempt to refute earlier experiments by the American, Edward L. Thorndike which suggested that animals are planless creatures that generate only random responses when confronted with a problem. According to this view, subhuman organisms "solve" a problem only when some trial-and-error behavior gains in strength as a result of being followed by reinforcement. Köhler's observations led him to question this view. He suggested that if the relevant objects were clearly presented, animals could solve problems insightfully by seeing the relationships between items. Once an animal had achieved an insightful solution, it would pass from random behavior to perfect performance in one trial, and would not have to rely on improving gradually, reinforcement by reinforcement, as suggested by Thorndike.

On what did Köhler base this conclusion? In one experiment he placed his most intelligent chimpanzee, Sultan, in a cage. Inside the cage was a stick and outside the cage a banana. Sultan first tried to grasp the banana with his hand, but it was out of reach. Next he tried tearing at a piece of wire that projected from the netting of his cage. This too was in vain. Eventually Sultan picked up the stick and played with it. At one point he suddenly rushed to the bars with the stick, reached out, and swept in his prize. The change in behavior was sudden and complete, not slow and gradual.

On hearing of this work Pavlov objected, suggesting that Köhler had not controlled the past conditioning history of his chimpanzees. He judged that sudden insight without prior conditioning was impossible. There is some later evidence which suggests that Pavlov may have been right in his analysis of this test. In 1945 the American psychologist Herbert G. Birch placed a laboratory-raised chimpanzee in a cage with food outside it beyond his reach. A rake of sorts was in perfect position for drawing in the food. Only one of six chimps seemed to arrive at a truly "insightful" solution in this pat situation. As it turned out, this chimp had had previous experience with many rakelike objects. In an attempt to produce relevant past conditioning as suggested by Pavlov, Birch allowed his other chimps free play for some time with sticks. After this play experience the chimps very quickly gave insightful solutions to the rake problem. It seemed that insight in this situation depended in large part on previous experience with sticks and rakes. It is as if the chimps had to learn what sticks and rakes are useful for before they could show an insightful solution to this problem.

An instructive analogy may be drawn between these relatively simple insight experiments with animals and experiments on more complicated problem solving with human beings. Max Wertheimer completed a series of problem-solving experiments in which subjects had to solve such problems as finding the area of a parallelogram. For Wertheimer, the key to solving a problem was discovering the "inner relations" of the situation and then reorganizing the situation in light of that discovery. For example, suppose a child who is capable of finding the area of a rectangle is asked to find the area of a parallelogram. Wertheimer claimed that if the child thinks about it, he will notice that a parallelogram is different from a rectangle because it has a "bump" on one side and a "gap" on the other (see Figure 1–5). Once this is noticed, the child will then realize that the "bump" and the "gap" are equivalent, and he will have discovered the "inner relations" of the situation. If he moves the "bump" so that it fills in the "gap," the parallelogram is converted to a rectangle of the same base and altitude. On this basis, the child has recognized the situation in light of his discovery. Now he knows that the formula for the area of a parallelogram is the same as it is for a rectangle.

Norman R. F. Maier has been responsible for devising a number of ingenious methods for studying how human adults attack problems. One

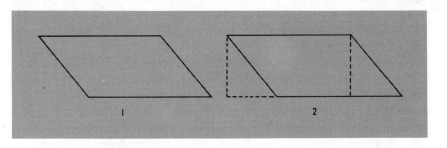

FIGURE 1–5. Wertheimer's parallelogram problem. The parallelogram (1) is equal in area to a rectangle of the same base and altitude because the "bump" at one end is equal to the "gap" at the other end (2). Adapted from M. Scheerer, *Scientific American* 208 (1963): 118.

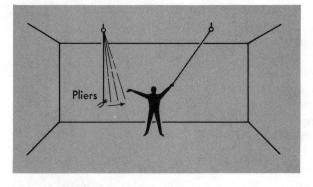

FIGURE 1–6. The two-rope problem. The object is to join the ropes. One solution is to tie pliers to the end of one of the ropes and set it swinging.

of these is depicted in Figure 1–6. In this technique, a subject is asked to tie two ropes together, using anything available in the room. There are a number of solutions possible; the difficulty is that while holding one rope he normally cannot reach the other. An elegant solution consists of tying pliers which are present to the end of one rope and setting the rope swinging. By catching it while holding the second rope the ropes may be knotted. In a variation on this method, Abe J. Judson, Charles N. Cofer, and Sidney Gelfand attempted to provide subjects with associations that could be used to facilitate insight. They preceded the subjects' experience of the two-string problem with some paired-associate learning. For some subjects one of the stimulus words in the list was *rope* and its response was *swing*; other subjects learned to respond to *rope* with *hemp*. The individuals with the relevant previous training (*rope–swing*) were more likely to arrive at the "swinging" solution. These experiments suggest the importance of the role previous learning plays in higher mental processes. It is clear that certain fundamental prior learning is crucial. The ability to use such prior learning determines how easily and effectively higher mental processes such as problem solving will be carried on.

In presenting this research sampler, we have tried to give you a feeling for the breadth of material covered and the subjects studied by researchers in the field of learning. In the following chapter, we shall step back from these specific instances and descriptions of research and try to present some of the underlying similarities in terms of common elements. We shall also get a picture of how a research problem in learning is planned and designed and how it is carried through to the final results.

The Language
And Methods
Of Learning

chapter two

The Use of Animals

Chapter 1 presented some examples of research in the area of learning—from conditioning planaria to human problem solving. You may wonder about the relationship between these extremes. Is there a continuum in learning from simple creatures to man? Although we can hardly imagine presenting complex problems to planaria, we do know that it is quite simple to condition responses in human beings. Furthermore, certain basic laws of conditioning seem to hold true as we move from one species to another. In fact, we find that many of the fundamental laws of learning that we derive from research on lower animals apply as well to man.

Why, then, does so much research use lower organisms, such as rats or dogs, as subjects? There are many reasons. For one thing, some scientists who study learning just prefer to work with animals because animals are their major interest. For another, this type of work feeds on itself. There is a thick notebook concerned exclusively with psychological research on the white rat. So much is known about the behavior of this ubiquitous and unlikely animal that an investigator studying simple learning in the rat has much of his or her background work already completed and can immediately focus on the specific problems now of interest.

In many cases learning researchers use simpler organisms such as rats when it would be immoral, illegal, or simply inconvenient to use people. There are countless examples of research in which the experimental nature of the work precludes or prohibits using human subjects. Consider the work of Frank Beach, who studied the effects on sexual behavior of taking out various amounts of brain tissue. As much as 75 percent of the cortex in male rats was removed, and then their sexual behavior was observed. As Beach removed more and more brain tissue, he found that the number of rats copulating during a test period declined dramatically. After two-thirds of the cortex had been removed, sexual behavior in the male rat was totally abolished. Interestingly, the brain plays a less important role in the sexual behavior of female rats, since, given an acceptable partner, they were still able to copulate with as much as 70 percent of their cortexes removed. Obviously, no sensible human being would agree to participate as a subject in one of these experiments; clearly, important work such as this could not be done on human subjects, and animal work is the only recourse.

Another reason for using lower organisms in research is that their history of conditioning and learning can be controlled. In Birch's experiment with chimpanzees we saw the advantage of observing an animal with a relatively controlled history. As you will recall, one of the six chimpanzees solved the problem on the first try. Birch notes that this chimpanzee was the only one that had had extensive experience in handling sticks in his preexperimental daily life. In an experiment that stretches over days and weeks it is often crucial to control the extra-experimental experiences of the subject; on this basis, animals in cages win out once again.

There is one more reason for using lower animals in learning research —and this is one that grew out of nonresearch considerations. The classical philosophical method of studying human beings consisted in the main of intuitive and searching self-explorations and thoughtful consideration of the behavior of others. Adopting Descartes's dualistic notion about the separation of human beings into mind and body, early students of human behavior restricted their attention to an analysis of the "conscious contents" of the mind, leaving the body to physiology. In the first quarter of this century, a group of psychologists led by James B. Watson aggressively rejected any attempt to study such unmeasurable and secret things as thoughts or feelings. The reason these *behaviorists* did this was that they were interested in making psychology more "scientific"; they set out, self-consciously and quite deliberately, to "build" a science. And so they limited themselves to the study of tangible events that could be seen in the plain light of day and could be measured. No one dared to use the words *mind* or *thought* in the laboratory of J. B. Watson. Thoughts are not tangible or easily measurable, but a rat's running speed in a maze is. In addition, when we put a human being into a simple learning situation involving a response such as an arm movement, he is always thinking, and these thoughts, unmeasurable as they are, constitute an unknown quantity in the experiment. If a rat is thinking while running down a maze, at least he cannot embarrass us by telling us about it. These considerations led psychologists studying learning at the beginning of this century to work with animals, and this seems to have brought the white rat into vogue; it was short on thought but long on ability to run a maze. Since then, however, we have devised methods for the scientific study of the thinking itself.

One more point. If we wish to know how a human being learned an arm movement before he or she could "think" about it, we must study organisms that do not already possess complex symbolic habits. For this purpose investigators turned first to lower animals and then to children.

A caution: we can never blindly assume that findings from animal research apply to human beings. Any specific research findings using animals must first be checked out with people. Where such findings cannot be checked on human beings because of the danger or discomfort of the procedures, generalization must be restricted since it will be based on indirect evidence. Why this concern with generalizing from animal research to humans? One of the things that scientists treasure most in their research and theory is elegance. One of the important components of elegance is parsimony. Parsimony is a rule of science which maintains that the world and its actions should be explained in the fewest possible number of laws. Clearly, if we can explain the behavior of both animals and men with the same set of laws, we are being parsimonious.

What Is Learning?

EXAMPLES OF UNLEARNED BEHAVIOR

Instincts, imprinting, and innate following.　Nearly all adult human behavior is learned. Some behavior, however, is reflexive or inborn: we breathe, our heart pumps, our cells apparently teem with activity, our knees jerk. All of this takes place without the benefit of learning. As we move to lower animals, reflexes and instincts account for more and more of their behavior. An instinct, according to R. Haber (1966), is "a pattern of behavior, usually complex in nature (to distinguish it from a reflex), which is found universally among the members of a species, occurs without the need for prior learning or experiences, is relatively invariant in form, and is reliably elicited or released by a particular and usually very simple stimulus."

There is sometimes the danger that a learning psychologist (one specializing in the field of learning) will consider as learned some complex behavior that is actually instinctive. Take the baby duck. Ducklings usually tend to follow their mothers. It would be rather easy for the learning psychologist to explain this behavior as learned: the duckling follows its mother because it has often been reinforced for doing so. It has been demonstrated, however, that this behavior is instinctive. At a certain crucial time, some hours after emerging from their shells, newborn ducklings can be induced to waddle after anything from a football to an experimenter that is moving nearby. This is accomplished by simply exposing the duckling to a moving object. If the timing is right, from then on they will continue to follow these objects. This behavior, called *imprinting*, is not learned, but is rather a kind of instinct reaction that capitalizes on a tendency which appears when the time is ripe. It is the "following" behavior that is innate—not the choice of what is followed. A duckling hatched in an incubator and exposed about fifteen hours afterward to a nonliving moving object for fifteen minutes will become imprinted on this object. In other words, it will follow the object as though it were its mother, and will continue to follow it in preference to other, real ducks. For the rest of its life the response of following will be elicited only by this kind of object.

Releasing stimuli and "released" behavior. Ethologists, who study comparative behavior such as imprinting, have observed even more complex unlearned behaviors. Let us examine one in some detail. The subject of this examination is the stickleback, a small, unobtrusive freshwater fish named after the bony spines extending from its back and which is remarkable for its behavior patterns of courtship, mating, and defense. The male begins his courtship by constructing an underwater nest. In order to make this nest into a home, the male stickleback has to attract a suitable female. He approaches female fish only if they are receptive; female sticklebacks advertise this condition by exhibiting a swollen abdomen. The male, in turn, communicates his interest by developing a red underbelly and by performing an intricate, zigzag dance. During this courtship period, the male stickleback defends the nest against other sexually active males, who are easily recognized by their red undersides. No red underbelly, no attack.

A series of experiments has shown that the occurrence of these complicated acts depends on specific stimuli in the environment of the stickleback. Thus, a mature male will make a sexual approach to a dummy fish, but only if the dummy has a swelling in the area of the abdomen. Dummies that resemble normal females but without swollen bellies get no attention at all. If the dummy has a red underbelly, it need not resemble the male stickleback much; in other words, the sexually mature male will attack dummies that bear little resemblance to other sticklebacks, provided they have red underbellies (see Figure 2–1).

All this highly complex social behavior is carried off successfully even though a stickleback need never have learned it or seen other sticklebacks behaving in such a manner. This intricate behavior pattern is built into sticklebacks when they are hatched. All that is necessary to elicit it is the occurrence of the *releasing stimulus*—the red belly or the swollen abdomen. Given the releasing stimulus, the response sequence is a foregone conclusion.

This example of stickleback behavior is one of many cases in which a particular stimulus "releases" a kind of behavior characteristic of a

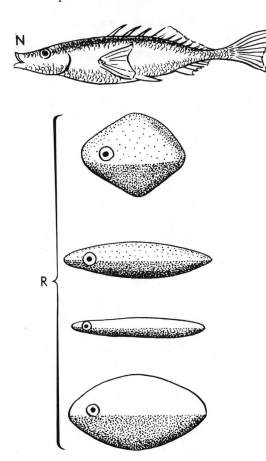

FIGURE 2–1. Dummies used to induce fighting in male sticklebacks. When a faithful model lacked the red underbelly (as in N) there was no attack. The models labeled R, which have red underbellies, all provoked fighting. (From V. G. Dethier and Eliot Stellar, *Animal behavior*, 2nd ed., Englewood Cliffs, N.J.: Prentice-Hall, 1964.)

species. The same concept is involved when the spot on the beak of a mother gull sets off a pecking response in her young children, which in turn causes the mother to regurgitate food for the children to eat. Releasers are generally very specific (a spot on a beak, a swollen abdomen); a spot or swelling in any other place won't serve as a releasing stimulus. This indicates that the behavior is controlled by a highly specific environmental event itself.

A DEFINITION OF LEARNING

We have devoted some space to stating what learning is not. What is it, then? Learning has a number of defining characteristics.

1. Learning may result in a change in behavior. We note a change in the planarian's response to the light. Now, when a light is presented, the animal contracts.

2. Learning comes about as a result of practice or experience. This characteristic eliminates sources of change such as illness and maturation.

3. Learning is a relatively permanent change. This characteristic eliminates changes in behavior that are temporary and easily reversible, such as those caused by extreme motivation. When you learn how to ride a bicycle, this is a permanent change. Even if you have not been on a bicycle for years, with just a few minutes' practice you can become quite proficient again. Continued practice at this task, however, might result in fatigue and a change in performance. This change in behavior as a result of practice would not be considered learning, since it is not permanent. A little rest will bring the performance up to par again.

4. Learning is not directly observable. Herein lies the crucial difference between learning and performance. The differentiating element is that you can *see* performance. To "see" learning you might have to cut subjects open somehow and look in the right place, at the right time, in the right way. At our present state of technological advancement this is impossible, and besides, doing this spoils subjects for other things. Learning is only one of the many variables influencing performance.

Despite the differences between learning and performance, the only way to study learning is through some observable behavior. In research we often try to subtract the effects of all irrelevant variables by the use of a *control group*. If we are studying the effect of amount of *work* on speed of learning a maze, we might study rats with high hunger motivation running in a maze with a heavy load strapped to their backs. Despite the complicating effects introduced by the high motivation, we need it in order to get the rats to run in the maze. For a control group we may study a group of litter mates running in the maze with identical hunger motivation but with only a pack of balsa wood on their backs.

When we subtract the balsa-wood-group's results from the heavy-pack-group's results, we must ascribe any difference in maze performance to the effect of the heavy load, since otherwise the groups are identical. May we now say we have observed differences in learning? No! These are only differences in performance. If we want to study learning we must now test both groups of rats in the maze either without any packs or with both groups wearing identical heavy or light packs (we would probably split our original groups and try all three). If we now find no differences in maze-running ability, then we can deduce that although amount of work has an effect on performance, it has no effect on learning.

The Language of Learning

We have already pointed out that we can never really observe learning; we see only what precedes performance, the performance itself, and the consequences of performance. Before proceeding to the complexities of this process, it might be worthwhile to pause and define some terms that relate to these three observable events.

WHAT PRECEDES PERFORMANCE

What precedes an act we usually call a *stimulus*. Stimuli can be as arresting and complex as the activities of an Egyptian bellydancer, or as boring and simple as a pure tone of moderate frequency and intensity. Pragmatically, it is often useful to distinguish stimuli that clearly originate outside an organism from those that come from within. Feelings of being thirsty or hungry are internal stimuli, while *proprioceptive* is the term applied to internal stimuli resulting from muscle movement. We are usually unaware of most of the internal stimulation that regulates our behavior. Did you realize that you were breathing fifteen minutes ago and that this breathing was producing internal stimuli?

We measure stimuli. We use foot-candles to measure the brightness of a light; pounds per square inch to measure the intensity of pressure of a touch; decibels to measure the loudness of a tone; volts and amperes to measure the intensity of a shock; and wavelength to measure the hue of a light. It is clear that some stimuli are harder to measure than others—say, rumblings from a stomach. If pushed, though, we would try even to measure the number and strength of stomach rumblings. When we move away from physical dimensions the method of measurement changes. We can easily measure the size of a nonsense syllable, but what about its meaningfulness? As we pointed out in Chapter 1, we estimate this by the number of words or ideas a syllable suggests to judges. If we specify carefully the conditions of the judgments, such as the instructions given to the judges, we have a useful definition of the meaningfulness of nonsense syllables. Indeed, we *would* specify all these determinants of meaningfulness to promote clear communication. Since we specify the operations or procedures involved, this type of definition is called an *operational definition*. We could define the meaningfulness of a nonsense syllable in nonoperational terms—for instance, the feeling of "wordness" that the nonsense syllable conveys. But since this statement does not tell us how to go out and measure meaningfulness, it is not an operational definition. In a sense, once we have operationally defined meaningfulness, further usage of the word is often only an abbreviated way of restating the operations of measurement. The major purpose of operational definitions is to promote clarity of communication.

This important function of operational definitions is clearly brought out by a consideration of another type of variable that usually precedes performance—motivation. If we were content to describe our experimental subjects as simply highly motivated, or very hungry, or quite desirous, our communication would not be precise. But we can operationally define a very hungry rat as one that has been starved for a specified number of hours after having been permitted to eat his fill.

THE PERFORMANCE ITSELF

The second stage of performance we call the *response*. A response can be as complex as trying to rub your stomach in a circular motion with your left hand while patting your head with your right, or as simple as a twitch of a muscle in your forehead. Responses come in any size; but when they get to be highly complex, such as turning on lights, closing shades, and turning up the heat, we usually call them *acts*. Like stimuli, responses can be relatively overt (screaming at the top of your lungs) or relatively covert (sweating). Both of these responses are measurable: we measure the loudness of the scream in decibels, or the amount of sweating by passing a small and undetectable electric current through the skin ("undetectable" meaning the subject can't feel it at all, yet it is measurable)—when a person sweats the current passes through the skin more easily. This change in current flow, which can be detected by instruments, is called the *galvanic skin response*, GSR (or sometimes the psychogalvanic response, PGR).

A response almost inevitably becomes in turn a stimulus. If you respond to a stimulus with fear, you may sense your heartrate increasing, your blood pressure rising, your extremities getting cold and sweaty, and your breathing growing shallow. If you pay attention when you turn this page you will notice that your arm movements produce proprioceptive stimuli. The fear and the arm movements are responses that produce stimuli (such as muscle tension) hence the term *response-produced stimuli*. Furthermore, we can learn responses to response-produced stimuli.

If methods already exist, such as for meaningfulness of syllables or for loudness of tones, the measurement of stimuli in a laboratory is usually not difficult, since the experimenter is the one who originates the buzzer or the shock. He knows what is coming and can either measure it beforehand or prearrange conditions so that he records or measures it during the experiment. But problems of measurement occur even with stimuli. Take the case of operant conditioning of the mental patient by the college student. The latter did not know what stimuli preceded the response he was conditioning; he simply waited for the response and then reinforced it. It is clear that in some kinds of learning research stimuli will be difficult (some think unnecessary) to specify.

But we almost always must measure the response. Suppose we have a T-maze with shock apparatus in it, and we shock an animal each time it goes to the right arm of the maze. At some point we turn on the shock and look to see whether the animal learned to run to the island of safety in the left arm of the maze. If our point is, say, to detect the difference in effect of two levels of shock, we must measure the response as precisely as possible in order to know what effects different levels of shock have had. There are several major types of measurement available. The simplest measure is merely a count of the number of times the "correct" response (turning left in the T-maze and reaching the island of safety) occurs in a given number of trials. Thus, we can say that under shock level A a rat made the correct response in eight of ten trials; under shock level B he made the correct response in only three out of ten trials. This measure is called the *frequency* of response. We can also measure the amount of time it takes a response to get underway. We could put an electric-eye device at the exit of the starting box and wire a clock to turn on when the electric shock begins and stop when the rat, in leaving the starting box, interrupts the photoelectric beam. We call this measure the *latency* of response. In addition, we could have another clock wired to start with the electric shock and to stop when the rat reaches the island of safety. This would record *speed of response*, or *response time*. On some trials the rat may turn right instead of left; this would be an *error*. We can also measure the percentage of mistakes that occur. The percentage of correct responses and the percentage of errors give you the same information—except when the rat does not leave the starting box. We may also want to know how "large" a response is. An experimenter once harnessed rats to a pulley-and-string device that measured the force of the rats' pull. He then varied the rats' motivation and measured the resultant differences in strength of pull as each rat left the starting box of the maze. This measure is called the *amplitude* of the response. After conditioning we sometimes wish to know how strong the conditioned response is. In the case of the planarian we could continue to present the light but omit the electric shock; the strength of the conditioned habit would be reflected by the number of trials on which the animal continues to respond to the light alone.

In operant conditioning we often measure the *rate of response*. As the college student reinforced the mental patient with candy for facing the door to the stairway, the patient turned to face the door more and more regularly. In the first hour he faced the door "hardly at all"; in the second hour "a little bit"; in the third hour "fairly often"; finally he faced it "almost all the time." In short, the rate of the door-facing response increased. The rate of response is a particularly useful measure in operant conditioning situations. Since there is often no specific stimulus, it is hard to say when a trial begins; it is sensible, therefore, to count the *number of responses per unit of time.*

When we study the learning of word lists, we often measure the number of repetitions of the list before learning is completed; the "criterion for learning" is arbitrarily set at some level such as two or three consecutive perfect trials of the entire list. This measure is usually called "trials to criterion."

A CONSEQUENCE OF PERFORMANCE:
REWARD OR REINFORCEMENT

Operationally defined, a reward or *reinforcement* is an event that immediately follows a response and serves to increase the likelihood of that response. Here is a case where an operational definition must be tied down at both the stimulus end (an event) and at the response end (increases the likelihood of that response). "Events" that are rewarding for the white rat include escape from shock and the morsel of food at the end of the maze. These rewards might be used to increase the likelihood of such responses as jumping a hurdle or turning left in a T-maze.

There are four aspects of reward that we shall briefly consider: First, the reinforcement must be presented soon after the response occurs. If a reward, such as a delicious dog biscuit, precedes Fido's rolling over, or if Fido rolls over and is not given a biscuit until an hour later, he will not learn to connect the biscuit with the act of rolling over. This is known as the principle of *temporal contiguity*. The second point is that in order for reinforcement to be effective, the animal must pay *attention* to it. If the dog does not see the biscuit or is busy doing something else, the biscuit will not increase the likelihood of a rolling-over response.

The third point is that the dog must *want* the biscuit; if he has just gobbled down a full-course meal of Friskies, he may not be interested in an additional biscuit. This point touches on the topic of *motivation*, which will be covered in Chapter 5. The fourth point is that the response must be a part of the animal's repertoire of responses. A pound of biscuits will not induce a dog to dial the telephone.

With animals, the rewards used in experiments are usually chosen to reduce some physiological need. A male rat completing a maze finds, depending on what he has been deprived of, a receptive female, food, water, or escape from an electric shock.

In the course of investigating the effect of direct electrical stimulation of the brain upon a rat's behavior, James F. Olds and Peter Milner accidentally discovered a novel way to deliver a reward. The electrical stimulation is provided by a tiny electrode implanted deep in the brain (Figure 2–2). One day, unknown to the experimenters, the placement of the electrode in one historic rat was slightly off target. The experimenters noted that when the rat was placed in an open field and stimulated (there is no pain at all associated with such stimulation), he tended to return repeatedly to the spot where he had been stimulated.

> More stimulation at that place caused him to spend more of his time there. Later we found that this same animal could be pulled to any spot in the maze by giving a small electrical stimulus *after* each response in the right direction. This was akin to playing the hot and cold game with a child. Each correct response brought electrical pulses which seemed to indicate to the animal that it was on the right track. [J. Olds and P. Milner. Positive reinforcement produced by electrical

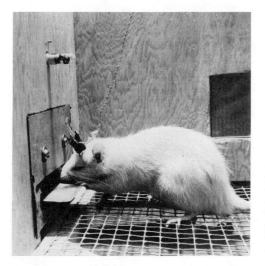

FIGURE 2–2. This rat, with an electrode implanted in his brain, has been placed in a Skinner box where his bar-pressing responses can be manipulated by electrical stimulation of the "pleasure" center of the brain. (Courtesy of Dr. James Olds.)

stimulation of septal area and other regions of rat brain. *J. comp. physiol. Psychol.*, 47 (1954): 419–27.]

In effect, what Olds and Milner had discovered was a place in the brain that acts as a reward center. In any case, after stimulation the preceding response increased in likelihood, which, by our definition, makes it a reward. They tested further and found that even if starved an animal would pass up food in order to receive electrical stimulation. The rat learned to run in a T-maze to receive the stimulation. For rats, such stimulation is completely irresistible. If allowed to press a bar as often as it wants with this electrical stimulation as the only reward, a rat will continue to press it at the fantastic rate of up to eight thousand times an hour—until sheer exhaustion or severe dehydration force an interruption.

Where in the brain is this pleasure center? When the rat was killed and its brain microscopically examined, it was found that the electrode was in a portion of the brain called the *anterior commissure*. In subsequent research, the investigators have discovered that only very circumscribed areas of the brain produce a "reward" effect. Other areas are quite neutral; still other areas produce a "punishment" effect. Long after Olds and Milner's initial discovery, when the probing techniques became refined and polished, some psychologists discovered that human brains also possess pleasure centers. What does it feel like to have your pleasure center stimulated? Dr. Robert Heath claims that for one of his patients "the feeling was 'good'; it was as if he were building up to a sexual orgasm." Research on these matters is in its early stages, but even now it is exceptionally exciting, for it promises to help us understand why rewards reward.

This chapter has introduced you to the methods, language, and thinking of researchers in the many fields of learning. We are now ready for a detailed examination of one of the many important, simple building blocks of learning: classical conditioning.

Simple Learning

CLASSICAL AND OPERANT
CONDITIONING

chapter three

Classical Conditioning

Around the turn of the present century, Ivan Pavlov discovered the conditioned response. Like so many other great discoveries, it happened almost by accident and didn't seem like much of a discovery at the time. What happened in Pavlov's laboratory was that in the course of a series of studies on gastric secretions in dogs, he noticed that the sound of a caretaker's approaching footsteps tended to evoke the flow of saliva in his dogs. What was important about this was that the dogs salivated well before food was put in their mouths. On the basis of this observation, Pavlov decided to stop working on gastric secretions (work for which he had already won a Nobel Prize) in order to make a systematic study of this new reaction which he called a "psychic secretion." Rather than continue to work with footsteps as a stimulus, he now trained dogs to salivate to a tuning fork or to a light.

Even with this change, Pavlov's observations don't seem to be earth-shattering or overwhelming; surely, we all have noticed the same thing when we only think about eating a steak or some other food we like. What, then, was so important about these observations that Pavlov changed the direction of his life's work? And—perhaps even more importantly—why has psychology come to accept them as great discoveries?

There are two things that mark these observations as important: (1) for the first time, it was possible to talk about how a part of the physical environment (e.g., a tuning fork) came to be associated with and control an animal's response; and (2) for the first time it also was possible to do this in perfectly objective and nonmental ways. Before Pavlov, a number of philosophers, most notably Locke and Hobbes, had talked about the development of the mind in terms of the association of ideas. Perhaps Locke expressed it best when he compared the human mind to a blank tablet on which the environment writes its message in the form of ideas. According to an associationistic viewpoint—as this philosophy was called—one idea leads to another because in the past these two ideas occurred together in terms of either time or space. This principle of mental operation is called the *law of contiguity*, which in its most clearcut version simply says that two ideas come to mind at the same time because they have occurred together—that is, in contiguity—in the past.

But ideas are invisible, and psychology deals in observables. Like Rumpelstiltskin, it was Pavlov's genius to turn the philosopher's straw (ideas) into the psychologist's gold (responses). From the very beginning, Pavlov saw his work as having to do with "psychic secretions," and when the concept of the conditioned response became popular in the United States it was always considered both as an important piece of data and as an important insight as to how animals learn. With the law of contiguity in mind, and classical conditioning procedures in the laboratory, psychology was ready to answer the question: how do organisms learn?

As we shall soon see, the answer to this question took a number of different forms, but one that has always interested psychologists has to do with a careful analysis of Pavlov's procedure, or what has come to be called *classical conditioning*. Such careful analysis was undertaken largely because classical conditioning was seen as both an important experimental procedure and as an important theoretical vehicle for "bringing the mind into being."

THE FATE OF CONDITIONED RESPONSES

If pairing a bell with food comes to produce an anticipatory response to the bell alone, what happens if only the bell is presented and never again paired with food? Descriptively the answer is simple enough: the dog stops salivating to the bell. This process is called *extinction*. Despite this obvious outcome, the actual results of a number of different studies are a good deal more complicated than this description would suggest. For one thing, it may take as many as thirty pairings to produce one drop of saliva during original learning, while one or two nonpaired trials may reduce the number by a quarter or a half. Secondly, if a conditioned response has been conditioned and extinguished, and if the animal is taken out of his harness and out of the experimental situation for a reasonable period of time say, an hour or so, when he is brought back into the situation and again presented with the bell the conditioned response reappears spontaneously at about half its strength prior to extinction. This phenomenon is called *spontaneous recovery*. If an animal is extinguished a second time, and a second rest period provided, he will again show spontaneous recovery when brought back to the laboratory for a third, fourth, or fifth time, depending on the number of initial pairings of bell with food and depending on the time interval between extinction and recovery periods. If an animal is continually put through the cycle of extinction and recovery, the spontaneous recovery that occurs becomes less and less after each cycle. Eventually, the response will not recover at all.

There are two other facts that seem to complicate what should be a simple picture. If a novel or unexpected stimulus is introduced while an experimenter is trying to extinguish a conditioned response, a temporary increase in the strength of the faltering conditioned response occurs. Because Pavlov believed that conditioned responses were only *inhibited* during extinction and not irretrievably lost, he believed that the introduction of a novel stimulus served to remove this inhibition. For this reason he gave the name *disinhibition*—release from inhibition—to the sudden rise in strength of a conditioned response undergoing extinction.

Running parallel to this surprising fact of extinction is a surprising fact of acquisition called *external inhibition*. In this case, if the experimenter introduces an extra noise simultaneously with, or just following, the bell or conditioned stimulus, the strength of the conditioned response will be markedly reduced on that trial. Because this type of disruption occurs so easily, Pavlov early found it necessary to do conditioning studies in soundproof rooms.

We can now trace the conditioned response through four stages: conditioning, extinction, rest, and spontaneous recovery. Figure 3–1 presents a schematic outline of this process. Note that we have included a number of rest and extinction periods after the initial conditioning and extinction period. In addition, note that the initial amount of spontaneous recovery decreases after each extinction period.

These, then, are some of the major phenomena of simple classical conditioning. Before the picture is complete, however, one more set of results has to be considered, and this concerns the time interval sepa-

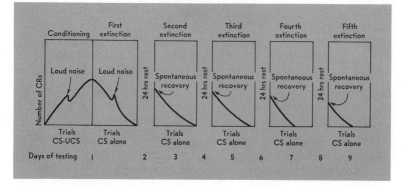

FIGURE 3–1. Stages in the conditioning and extinction of a conditioned response.

rating the conditioned stimulus (the bell) and the unconditioned stimulus (the meat powder). Since classical conditioning was often thought to provide an experimental procedure for understanding how the law of contiguity works, such an interest is quite reasonable.

VARIATIONS ON THE THEME:
TEMPORAL RELATIONS BETWEEN CS AND UCS

Up to this point we have considered only the case where the unconditioned stimulus occurs either at the same time as, or just following, the onset of the conditioned stimulus. This type of conditioning is called *simultaneous conditioning*. But beyond this, nearly all possible time relations have been used in conditioning research. Each has a name, as the diagrams in Figure 3–2 show. The top line in each part indicates the conditioned stimulus. A rise in this line denotes the onset of the conditioned stimulus. The lower line of the pair indicates the unconditioned stimulus, and here too a rise indicates the onset of the unconditioned stimulus. A drop in a line indicates the termination of each stimulus.

Which of these experimental setups leads to the easiest learning of a conditioned response? As you might expect, the simultaneous condition is best, but what might be surprising is that exact simultaneity of conditioned stimulus and unconditioned stimulus does not produce the fastest conditioning. Virtually all investigators have reported that a delay of about half a second between the onset of a conditioned stimulus and the onset of an unconditioned stimulus produces the fastest learning. On either side of this interval conditioning proceeds more slowly. In an early experiment involving these time relations, Helen M. Wolfle found that

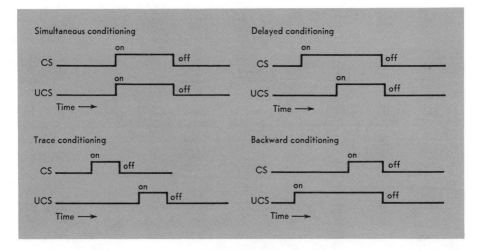

FIGURE 3–2. Relationship between CS and UCS in four types of conditioning.

having the conditioned stimulus precede the unconditioned stimulus by 0.5 second was best. The most complete study on this topic was that of A. Spooner and W. M. Kellogg, who worked with the following five temporal intervals between conditioned stimulus and unconditioned stimulus: −0.5 sec, −0.25 sec, +0.5 sec, +1.0 sec, and +1.5 sec (the negative numbers indicate *backward conditioning* when the unconditioned stimulus preceded the conditioned stimulus). In Figure 3–3 we see a composite of the results obtained by Wolfle and by Spooner and Kellogg. Again we see that the optimal interval between the conditioned stimulus and unconditioned stimulus is about +.5 sec. This persistent and specific time relation, intriguing as it is, has thus far eluded complete explanation.

HIGHER-ORDER CONDITIONING
AND TV ADVERTISING

There is one type of TV commercial that has been around for a long time and takes the general form: (1) Somebody (2) does something with (3) some product. For example, (1) Mickey Mantle (2) washes with (3) Dial. In actual commercials of this type, Mrs. American Homemaker, Willie Mays, Brigitte Bardot, and Johnny Unitas, can, and have, appeared as the "somebody" washing with, smoking, wearing, or eating, Dial, Camels, Arnel shorts, or Wheaties. The mind boggles at the possibility that any given "somebody" might be paired with the wrong action and product—say, Mrs. American Homemaker smoking Wheaties. Very interesting, but not very healthy.

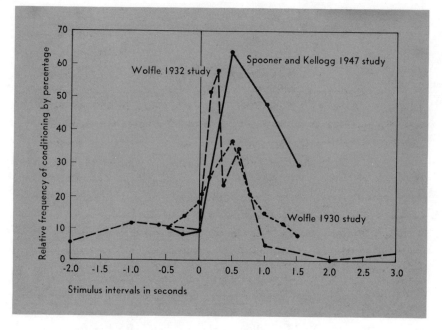

FIGURE 3–3. Comparison of the effectiveness of different CS-UCS intervals.
(From A. Spooner and W. N. Kellogg, *Amer. J. Psychol.*, 60 (1947): 327.)

Given this possible complication, why do advertisers continue to use this rather obvious approach? Whether advertisers realize it or not, they are implicitly assuming that the law of contiguity works in advertising as well as in classical conditioning. So, for example, we can consider the product name—often a nonsense word such as *Arnel* or *Lux*— as having very little in the way of original meaning; i.e., it is a perfect conditioned stimulus. The superstar—Mickey Mantle, Brigitte Bardot, etc.—can then be considered as analogous to an unconditioned stimulus with the positive meanings evoked equivalent to unconditioned responses. What the advertiser hopes to do is to transfer the set of emotional and other responses evoked by the star (unconditioned stimulus) to the product (conditioned stimulus). In this way, if part of the unconditioned response set evoked by Brigitte Bardot is that she evokes sexual feelings and meanings, then pairing her with a nonsense word such as *Arnel* should serve to connect such responses to the brand name and thereby induce the would-be consumer to buy Arnel shorts because they are likely to make you feel sexy or have someone else find you sexy. All of this, of course, is done by classical conditioning.

Now, while this is a plausible hypothesis, is there any evidence to support it? Perhaps the most relevant studies bearing on this issue were done by Arthur and Carolyn Staats and their co-workers on the topic of the conditioning of meaning. The Staatses based their theoretical analysis on the phenomenon of *higher-order conditioning* first described by Pavlov. Higher-order conditioning begins with the establishment of a conditioned response—say, a dog salivating in response to a bell. Once this response has been firmly established, the bell is then paired with a second conditioned stimulus—say, a light. After a few trials, the light comes to evoke salivation, although it has never been paired directly with food. Conditioning has taken place on the basis of pairing a new stimulus with a conditioned stimulus that had already been conditioned to produce a given response. Actually, higher-order conditioning is easier to establish in response to an unpleasant stimulus such as shock. Since an interpretation of why and how shock produces conditioned responses will be handled in great detail later, let us now only point out that such conditioned responses are more easily used in higher-order conditioning and leave an interpretation until later.

Given the existence of higher-order conditioned responses, the Staatses reasoned that if you paired a nonsense syllable such as *gej* with a set of pleasant words such as *love, justice, sweet,* etc., the nonsense syllable will come to be rated as more pleasant than if you paired it with a set of unpleasant words such as *putrid, nasty, ugly,* etc. In fact, in one study, the Staatses were able to shift the meaning of nationalities (i.e., Japanese, Korean, etc.) on the basis of conditioning of meaning procedures, sometimes making them more pleasant and sometimes less pleasant.

Even if we assume that such conditioning does take place, can we then say that people so conditioned will behave any differently toward words that are rated as pleasant or unpleasant? Here an experiment by Pollio and Gerow is relevant; these investigators asked students to provide word associations to stimulus words that were rated as either pleasant or unpleasant. All subjects gave their responses out loud, and so it was possible to determine how long it took them to respond to each type of word. The results of this study were quite clear in showing that students responded much more rapidly to pleasant words than to unpleasant words. If these students were presented with a list of pleasant and unpleasant words and asked only to respond to the last word, they responded slightly more rapidly to a pleasant word that was preceded by other pleasant words than to a pleasant word presented alone. On the other hand, these subjects responded much more slowly to an unpleasant word preceded by a list of other unpleasant words than to a single unpleasant word presented alone. Finally, these experimenters showed that it took students much *longer* to respond to a pleasant word that followed a list of unpleasant words than to a pleasant word either presented alone or preceded by other pleasant words. They also found that it took much *less* time to respond to an unpleasant word that followed a list of pleasant words than it took to respond to the unpleasant word presented alone or preceded by a list of other unpleasant words. What this means is that pleasant words produce fast responding and unpleasant words produce slow responding. Transferring this to the advertising situation—if an advertisement serves to condition pleasant responses to an originally meaningless brand name, people will more readily buy the product than they would if either unpleasant or nonemotional responses are evoked by that brand name. Let the public beware: although you may feel like a champion after having eaten your Wheaties, don't go out and pick a fight with Mohammed Ali; he not only feels like a fighter, he really can fight.

CONDITIONING, ANXIETY, AND PSYCHOTHERAPY

In his research Pavlov almost always made use of a positive unconditioned stimulus such as food. W. von Bechterev, a Russian contemporary of Pavlov, initiated the study of electric shock, a noxious stimulus, as an unconditioned stimulus. In Bechterev's basic experiment he would touch a dog on the left rear paw (conditioned stimulus) then an electric shock would be administered to the right front paw (unconditioned stimulus), at which point the dog would automatically respond by flexing that paw (unconditioned response). After a number of pairings of conditioned stimulus and unconditioned stimulus, the conditioned stimulus would be presented alone and a flexion of the right front paw (conditioned response) would occur. On this basis, Bechterev established an S-R (stimulus-response) connection between a touch on the left rear paw (conditioned stimulus) and flexion of the right front paw conditioned response). In this situation the dog does not avoid the shock by flexing his paw. Experimenters have also studied the effect of a conditioned response that enables the dog to escape a shock. In this situation, it turns out that conditioning proceeds much more rapidly.

It is this latter situation—where it is possible to avoid the shock—that is of great practical interest. Consider the following situation used in a classic study by Watson and Rayner. A nine-month-old infant named Albert served as the subject. Initially, Albert was shown a tame white rat, which at first only aroused the child's curiosity. After Albert had a chance to examine the rat, the animal was removed from his sight. Then the rat was presented again, and at the same time the experimenter sounded an alarming noise (the pounding of a steel bar with a hammer) behind Albert. This noise frightened the boy and caused him to cry. After pairing the rat with the harsh noise for about five trials, the experimenters presented the rat alone. This time the sight of the rat was enough to make Albert cry.

If we substitute the Pavlovian terminology of conditioned stimulus for the rat, unconditioned stimulus for the harsh noise, and unconditioned response (and later conditioned response) for the child's crying, we have a model of how an infant might learn to fear something through conditioning. We can now positively answer the question: Can a negative stimulus such as shock or a harsh voice be used as an unconditioned stimulus to produce a conditioned response? We may further say that if an animal or person is unable to avoid a noxious unconditioned stimulus, he will then learn fear as the response to an originally neutral conditioned stimulus.

The troubles of poor little Albert did not come to end when the white rat was removed from his sight, for now not only did the sight of the white rat frighten him, but other objects such as a ball of cotton, or a rabbit, or a white mask also frightened him. Albert was not frightened by any object that did not resemble the white rat (say, a block of wood), but he was frightened by objects that were similar to it in some way (being white and fuzzy).

This experiment would have been of only passing interest—a hint as to how fear was learned—if not for a follow-up study done by Mary Cover Jones. In this experiment a three-year-old boy by the name of Peter was brought to Jones's laboratory because he was afraid of white rats, and this fear extended to rabbits, fur coats, cotton balls, etc.—in short, a natural replica of the Little Albert situation. Although Jones tried a number of different approaches to ridding Peter of his fear, the one that worked best was to pair the feared object, a rat, with a pleasant event—in this case, eating his favorite dessert. The specifics went as follows. First the caged rat was brought into the same room as Peter but moved away until Peter could tolerate its presence without whimpering. While Peter kept track of the rat out of the corner of his eye, he was plied with ice cream. The next day the rat moved a little bit closer while Peter happily ate. Notice that Peter was manifesting a "happiness" response in the presence of the rat and that this response is incompatible with crying. After a number of such sessions the rat and Peter were happily reunited. This technique is ideal for retraining children. One caution, however: the situation must be handled with finesse. Rather than teaching Peter to be happy with the rat, the experimenters might have caused him to fear the dessert.

The principle involved in this case is quite clear: find some response pattern that is incompatible with being afraid; then pair the stimulus evoking this pattern with the feared object, making sure that the incompatible response is evoked more strongly than the fear response (i.e., in the beginning keep the rat far away from the child). Once the fear response is extinguished, reintroduce the incompatible response with a slightly stronger version of the conditional stimulus, again making sure the incompatible response is stronger than the fear response. Over a number of presentations, the fear response will be unlearned and the conditional stimulus will cease to be feared.

Although this is a highly reasonable and highly successful process, it still took almost thirty-five years before anyone systematically tried to desensitize people to feared objects on the basis of such inhibitory conditioning procedures. The very first attempt in this regard was made by a South African psychiatrist (now at Temple Medical School in Philadelphia) by the name of Joseph Wolpe. Wolpe's basic hypothesis is quite simple: most cases of neuroses depend on the evocation of fear or anxiety in certain specific situations. In order to overcome this anxiety, it is only necessary to relax the patient first and then ask him to think of these anxiety-evoking situations. In order to make sure that relaxation is complete and stronger than the anxiety evoked by specific situations, Wolpe makes use of two procedures: (1) progressive relaxation and (2) the establishment of fear hierarchies.

Progressive relaxation is a procedure originally developed in the early 1940s by the psychologist Edmund Jacobson. In this procedure the patient is taught to relax all of the major and minor muscle groups in his body. Wolpe reports that such relaxation is accompanied by autonomic reactions that are opposite to reactions evoked by anxiety. For example, some patients show a drop in pulse rate from 120 to 80 under progressive relaxation, while others show an equally rapid drying of profusely sweating palms. Training in such relaxation is usually given to a patient during five to seven interviews so that he becomes very effective at relaxing on cue.

Once the patient is able to produce these anti-anxiety states, the next step involves finding out when and where he is made anxious. In order to do this, the patient is asked to establish a *fear hierarchy*—that is, a list of stimulus situations which evoke anxiety in the patient, with the most disturbing items at the top and the least disturbing at the bottom. For example, the following anxiety hierarchy was established for a patient who had a great fear of small places (claustrophobia).

1. Being stuck in an elevator. (The longer the time, the more disturbing.)

2. Being locked in a room. (The smaller the room and the longer the time, the more disturbing.)

3. Passing through a tunnel in a railway train. (The longer the tunnel, the more disturbing.)

4. Traveling in an elevator alone. (The greater the distance, the more disturbing.)

5. Traveling in an elevator with an operator. (The greater the distance, the more disturbing.)

6. Traveling by railway train. (The longer the journey, the more disturbing.)

7. Being stuck in a dress with a stuck zipper.

8. Having a tight ring on the finger.

9. Visiting and being unable to leave at will (for example, if engaged in a card game).

10. Being told of someone in jail.

11. Having polish on fingernails and having no access to remover.

12. Reading of miners trapped underground.

Therapy was done in the following way (In reading over this procedure, think again of Peter and his fear of rats, etc.): First the patient was told to relax as deeply as possible. She was then asked to imagine the weakest scene on the anxiety hierarchy—i.e., reading about miners trapped underground. If she felt disturbed by this, or any further scene, she was to indicate this to the therapist by raising her left index finger as a sign. If the patient raised her finger, she was told to stop imagining the scene for a short time period. If the patient did not raise her finger, she was then told to imagine the scene once more.

After three presentations without any finger raising, the patient moved on to the next scene in the hierarchy. This procedure was carried on until the patient could go on to the topmost level of the hierarchy. At this point, anxiety had been inhibited to stimuli which previously produced anxiety and the patient should be able to stand the topmost scene when she comes across it in reality. According to Wolpe and other learning-theory therapists, this turns out to be true in the vast majority of their cases.

GENERALIZATION

The use of an anxiety hierarchy by behavior therapists such as Wolpe works on a logic exactly the reverse of that we observed in the case of Little Albert. As you may remember, Little Albert, who was conditioned to fear a white rat, generalized his fear to other objects that resembled the white rat such as rabbits, cotton balls, etc. Such a response, based on stimulus similarity, is called *stimulus generalization*. As in the case of Albert, we find that after a response is trained to a stimulus, similar stimuli also come to elicit that response. In a very strict sense, generalization is always with us, since we never experience the same stimulus in exactly the same way more than once. Each time a person walks down the street and enters the front door to his house, his retina is doubtless stimulated in a different manner. This may be due to changes in light levels because of weather, time of day, or wearing sunglasses. It may be due to the exact angle at which he enters the street and approaches his house. In any case, he is responding to a "new" stimulus which is similar to the stimulus situation in which he learned his response—our defining condition for stimulus generalization.

The use of anxiety hierarchies points to a slightly different kind of stimulus generalization, one where we start with a response and define a wide variety of stimuli as similar because they evoke that same response. Obviously, all of the elements in a given hierarchy are not physically similar, what is similar is their meaning to the patient. Generalization based on learned similarity between stimuli is called *secondary-stimulus generalization*, so as to distinguish it from *primary stimulus generalization*. In this latter case, similarity between stimuli can be described in physical terms. Thus, the color orange is closer to red than it is to green, a note of 256 cps is closer to one of 260 cps than one of 290 cps; among sandpapers, grade 00 is more like grade 01 than grade 09; and so on.

There is one fact about generalized responses that is quite obvious and quite important: namely, that as stimuli become less similar (on the basis of either physical or learned equivalences) to the original conditioned stimulus, the responses they evoke are progressively weaker than the original conditioned response. It is precisely this fact that allowed Wolpe to develop a hierarchy of fear-evoking situations, with the situation least similar to the one actually feared evoking the weakest fear responses. If the patient has a morbid fear of being confined in an elevator, much less fear is evoked by reading about miners trapped underground.

While this hypothesis seems to be quite reasonable, and appears to work quite well in the clinic, what do the experimental facts look like? Although Watson and Rayner (1920) did the classic study on this topic, it remained for later investigators to quantify this phenomenon more precisely. In one early experiment, Pavlov applied a vibrating stimulus to the shoulder of a dog as a conditioned stimulus. This conditioned stimulus had been previously paired with food, and the number of drops of saliva produced in a thirty-second period was taken as a measure of the conditioned response. The results presented in Table 1 show the spatial pattern of generalization obtained and indicate that as the physical location of a test stimulus becomes more distant from the location

Table 1

Spatial Pattern of Stimulus Generalization in Dogs	
PLACE STIMULATED	NUMBER OF DROPS OF SALIVA IN 30 SECONDS
Front paw	6
Shoulder (CS)	8
Side near shoulder	7
Side near thigh	3
Thigh	0
Hind paw	0

From I. P. Pavlov, *Conditioned reflexes* (trans. by G. V. Anrep). London: Oxford Univ. Press, 1927.

of the original conditioned stimulus, the strength of the conditioned response decreases.

Marjorie Bass and Clark Hull conducted this same experiment with male college students. Instead of salivation they used the galvanic skin response (GSR) as the conditioned response. The GSR mentioned in Chapter 1 reflects a general state of emotionality, tension, or excitement. When we are emotional, our automatic nervous system becomes active. One of the results of such activity is increased sweating. Thus, as we become more emotional, we sweat; and as we sweat, the electrical resistance of our skin decreases. This decrease in skin resistance can be observed with proper instruments, so it has frequently been measured as a conditioned response. In the Bass and Hull study (as in Pavlov's) a vibration to the left shoulder was the conditioned stimulus. Immediately following the onset of this stimulus they administered an electric shock to the subject's right wrist and observed the conditioned GSR in the subject's left hand. After conditioning they tested for generalization by applying vibratory stimuli to the small of the student's back, left thigh, and left calf, each point exactly sixteen inches from the one nearest it. The amount of response elicited by each of these locations is shown in Figure 3–4. This curve is called the *gradient of stimulus generalization*.

Later studies have also found basically the same result using a wide variety of different stimuli as the conditioned stimulus. So, for example, some experimenters have used changes in the loudness or pitch of a tone, some have used changes in the area of rectangles, and some have even used nonsense syllables having a different number of letters in common. In all cases generalization occurred. As these results show, generalization is a highly robust phenomenon, one that should figure in a good deal of our thinking about a number of different phenomena not all of which are directly related to classical conditioning.

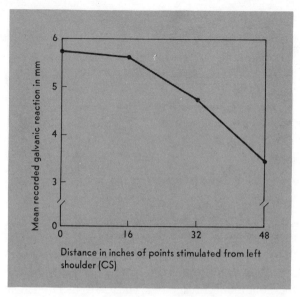

FIGURE 3–4. A gradient of stimulus generalization obtained by Bass and Hull. (From M. Bass and C. L. Hull, J. comp. Psychol., 1934).

STIMULUS GENERALIZATION AND THE
DISPLACEMENT OF EMOTION

The term *displacement* refers to the kind of behavior of a boy who goes home and shouts at his little sister after quietly taking a severe scolding by his teacher in school. It consists of transferring a response from an original target to one that is more available—or at least safer. If the sister then turns and kicks the dog, we have still another example of displacement. Displacement is a concept that has seen wide use in the study of personality; it was first noted by Sigmund Freud and later described in generalization terms by Neal Miller and his students. As a subject for this discussion, let us take a young lady's courtship problems. As will quickly become obvious, this analysis attempts to explain only one of the many influences on her courting behavior.

As any parent can tell you, the first object of a little girl's affection is her father. Her later reactions to men are in some degree influenced by the similarity of these men to her father. This reaction on the basis of similarity can be considered an instance of generalization. We might depict it in terms of a gradient as in Figure 3–5. (The gradient is depicted as a straight line for purposes of clarity in the more complex figures that follow.) The eyes in Figure 3–5 vary in terms of their similarity to the father's eyes. As a dimension of similarity we have arbitrarily chosen to consider only eye color in order to eliminate needless

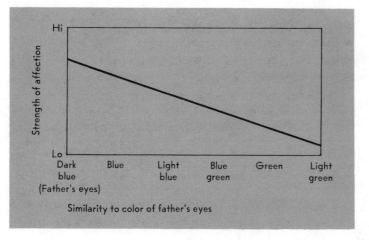

FIGURE 3–5. Stimulus generalization of a girl's affection response to her father.

detail. We could, of course, use any other important physical dimension, such as hair color, or height, or any more complex dimension such as friendliness or outgoingness. To be truly realistic, we would have to use some weighted average of all relevant dimensions.

If our young lady were presented with this array of men proposing marriage, which would she pick? To begin with, thoughts relating to the father's candidacy would be accompanied by massive anxiety because of our civilization's powerful incest taboos. Would her choice, then, be man 1? Well, because of man 1's great similarity to the father, he shares, through generalization, more of the anxiety avoidance relating to the incest taboo than the other suitors. The generalization gradient of this anxiety-avoidance response is shown along with the gradient for generalization of the approach response in Figure 3–6. Let us stop to point out a few features of this graph. To begin with, notice that the father elicits more avoidance than approach. This is in accordance with the dominance of the incest taboo. Notice also that the avoidance curve descends more rapidly (greater slope) than the approach curve. This is in accordance with results of research comparing the slopes of approach and avoidance generalization curves. In order to determine what she is likely to do, we must only subtract one gradient from the other at any point in question. She will choose the man whose resultant approach remainder is highest. In this case it is man 2.

DISCRIMINATION

Although generalization is of great help to people, unless controlled it can lead to difficulties. Take the case of a new lieutenant in the army

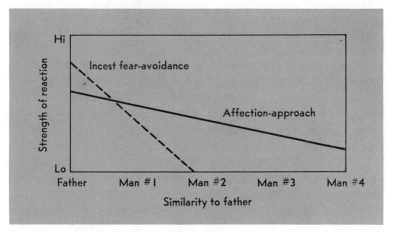

FIGURE 3–6. Interaction of generalization gradients of a girl's incest fear and affection response to her father.

who says, "Good morning, Captain," to the major. Although the uniform of a captain and major are similar, there are important differences that the new lieutenant must learn to distinguish, and quick! The bases of such *discrimination* have been carefully studied, with perhaps the clearest indication of what's going on presented in an old experiment by Hilgard, Campbell, and Sears (1938).

In this experiment subjects were conditioned by lighting up a panel on a board in front of them (conditioned stimulus) and then pairing this with a puff of air to the subject's cornea (unconditioned response). The conditioned response consisted of an anticipatory eye blink occurring in response to the conditioned stimulus alone. The conditioned response was established on the first day. The negative stimulus, introduced in random alternation with the positive conditioned stimulus on the second day, was lighting up a different panel on the board. This second stimulus was never paired with a puff of air to the eye. The results of this experiment for both day 1 and day 2 are presented in Figure 3–7. Perhaps the most important results are indicated at points *a* and *b*. Point *a* shows that when the negative stimulus was first introduced on day 2, subjects continued to produce a conditioned response, thereby showing stimulus generalization. With repeated experience, where only the positive conditioned stimulus was paired with an air puff and the negative one was not, the data presented at point *b* occurred: there was a marked difference in frequency of occurrence of the conditioned response given to both stimuli. This curve applies to a whole set of results dealing with the topic of discrimination.

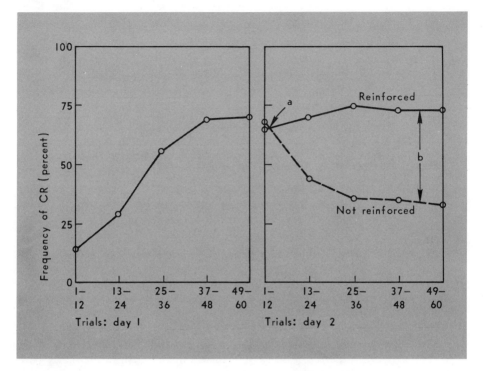

FIGURE 3–7. Discrimination learning in human subjects. (From E. R. Hilgard and D. G. Marquis, *Conditioning and learning* (New York: D. Appleton-Century Company, 1940), p. 186.

EXPERIMENTAL NEUROSIS

In the experiment by Hilgard, Campbell, and Sears, differences between the two stimuli were very great indeed. What would happen in this case if we required finer and finer discriminations? Here an early experiment by Pavlov is quite relevant and quite revealing. In this experiment Pavlov first trained a dog to discriminate a circle (as the positive stimulus) from an ellipse (as the negative one). The circle was always positive (followed by the UCS, meat powder). The ratio between the horizontal and vertical diameters of the ellipse began at 2:1. As the discrimination experiment progressed, the ellipse was brought closer and closer to the circle. When the ellipse ratio reached 9:8, dogs became extremely disturbed and disorganized. They also lost the benefit of all previous training and responded at random to either circle or ellipse. This condition has come to be called *experimental neurosis* by analogy to the disorganization of behavior that is often true of human neurosis.

In recent years the idea of experimental or learned neuroses has been emphasized most strongly by Wolpe and other behavior therapists. Wolpe's original experiments leading to the development of his therapy techniques were based on early studies of "experimental neuroses" done by Masserman at the University of Chicago in 1943. Masserman, using hungry cats, set up a situation in which the cats were trained to operate a switch that produced food. At the moment of feeding a shock was administered to the animal, thereby producing a conflict. Masserman's animals showed a number of "neurotic" symptoms such as (1) restlessness, (2) trembling, and rapid and irregular pulse and respiration, (3) refusal to eat, (4) stereotyped behavior, and (5) regressive behavior such as playfulness, preening, and other kitten-like characteristics.

Wolpe, because of his interest in getting rid of neurotic symptoms, used essentially the same procedure as Masserman in developing "neuroses" in cats. Once such "neuroses" were developed, he attempted to get rid of them by using the same procedure Mary Cover Jones had used with Peter—namely, feeding the animal first at a great distance from the box in which he was shocked and gradually moving the cat closer to the original box. Over a number of days, cats were again able to eat in the shock box; and thus the principle of reciprocal inhibition was first established for treating neurotic behavior in cats.

Although we have emphasized the similarities between human and animal neurotic behavior, we could also emphasize the differences between the restricted animal experiments and the potentially rich variety of neuroses brought about by the symbolic and verbal abilities of humans. Through secondary generalization the human being can find conflict in situations far removed from the area of original training. Despite these differences, there have been a number of useful attempts at understanding human neurotic behavior in terms of the basic laws of learning. In future years we have every reason to expect that many new treatment techniques will take their inspiration from work done in the learning laboratory.

Operant Conditioning

If classical conditioning grew in the fertile soil of a chance observation, so too did operant conditioning, at least if we accept the word of B. F. Skinner. According to Skinner (1959)—the first operant conditioner— the story goes something like this: when he was a graduate student, Skinner was interested in finding out how long it took rats to go back to a start box after they had gotten a reward at the other end of a straight alley. The original apparatus was built in the shape of an oblong with food in one corner and the start box in the opposite corner. But let's let Skinner tell it himself:

There was one annoying detail, however. The rat would often wait an inordinately long time at the food ramp before starting down the back alley on the next run. There seemed to be no explanation for this. When I timed these delays with a stop watch, however, and plotted them, they seemed to show orderly changes. This was, of course, the kind of thing I was looking for. But there was no reason why the runway had to be 8 ft. long. . . . I saw no reason why the rat could not deliver its own reinforcement.

A new apparatus was built. [In Fig. 3–8,] we see the rat eating a piece of food just after completing a run. It produced the food by its own action. As it ran down the back alley A to the far end of the rectangular runway, its weight caused the whole runway to tilt slightly on the axis C; and this movement turned the wooden disc D, permitting a piece of food in one of the holes around its perimeter to drop through a funnel into a food dish. The food was pearl barley—the only kind I could find in the grocery stores in reasonably uniform pieces. The rat had only to complete its journey by coming down the home stretch B to enjoy its reward. The experimenter was able to enjoy his reward at the same time, for he had only to load the magazine, put in a rat, and relax. Each tilt was recorded in a slowly moving kymograph.

Eventually, of course, the runway was seen to be unnecessary. The rat could simply reach into a covered tray for pieces of food, and each movement of the cover could . . . move a pen one step in a cumulative curve. The first major change in rate observed in this way was due to ingestion. Curves showing how the rate of eating declined with the time of eating comprised the other part of my thesis. But a refinement was needed. The behavior of the rat in pushing open the door was not a normal part of the ingestive behavior of *Rattus rattus*. The act was obviously learned, but its status as part of the final performance was not clear. It seemed wise to add an initial conditioned response connected with ingestion in a quite arbitrary way. I chose the first device

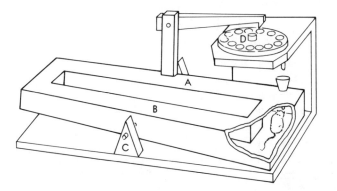

FIGURE 3–8. An early form of the Skinner box. (From B. F. Skinner, "A case history in scientific method," in S. Koch (ed.), *Psychology: a study of a science* (New York: McGraw-Hill Book Company, 1959), 364.

which came to hand—a horizontal bar or lever placed where it could be conveniently depressed by the rat to close a switch which operated a magnetic magazine. Ingestion curves obtained with this initial response in the chain were found to have the same properties as those without it.

Gradually, over the course of the next forty years, minor improvements were made in this apparatus so that at the present time most work done on operant conditioning is done in a small, sometimes air-conditioned, sometimes soundproofed box that contains a little lever, a food cup, and perhaps even a small light. This apparatus is called a *Skinner box*, after the man who invented it and first described the process of operant conditioning (see Figure 3–9). Typically, the lever in the Skinner box is connected to a recording pen. This pen rests and writes on a constantly moving strip of paper; when no response is occurring the pen simply draws a horizontal line. To record the occurrence of each lever response, the pen makes a small upward movement. When after many upward movements it reaches the top of the paper, it usually is automatically reset to the bottom of the page and can begin again. An example of the data generated by this apparatus is presented in Figure 3–10, which is called a *cumulative response graph*. Note that the ordinate (vertical axis) in Figure 3–10 denotes the total cumulative number of responses, whereas the abscissa (horizontal axis) presents a continuous record of time. There are four responses on this graph, each of which is indicated by an upward deflection. The graph shows many things. For one, obviously the time between responses 3 and 4 is shorter than the time between responses 1 and 2. For another, the steepness of the slope between any two points tells the rate of response. Here, the solid line labeled *A* denotes the slope between responses 1 and 2, while

"Boy, have I got this guy conditioned! Every time I press the bar down he drops in a piece of food."

FIGURE 3–9. A typical Skinner box? (Adapted, by permission from *Jester*, Columbia University.)

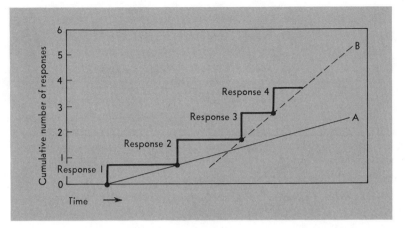

FIGURE 3–10. A typical cumulative response graph showing a record of the first four responses. A and B denote slope—hence, rate—of responses.

the dotted line labeled *B* denotes the slope between responses 3 and 4. Since the slope of line *B* is steeper than the slope of line *A*, the rate of response between 3 and 4 is faster than the rate between 1 and 2.

It is possible to compare differences in response rate for different animals with such graphs—*the steeper the slope the faster the response rate*. In Figure 3–11 we see graphs for two rats pushing a lever for food. Animal X's response rate is considerably faster than animal Y's rate, as is shown by the steeper slope of X's curve. Such a difference might result if X is hungrier than Y.

OPERANT CONDITIONING:
SOME EXPERIMENTAL FINDINGS

So far all we have described are the technical details of a simple piece of apparatus. The real question is: what kinds of results are possible given such a device? Perhaps the single most important discovery concerns the role of reward, or reinforcement, in behavior. It had been known for quite a long time in psychology—at least as long ago as the turn of the century, when Edward L. Thorndike did his classic studies on the role of rewards in learning—that animals would learn to do things if they were rewarded with food or water for doing these things. What had not been made clear, however, was how to describe the event that served to bring about these changes in behavior. Some like Thorndike spoke of reward in terms of alleviating an annoying condition; others like Clark Hull spoke of reward in terms of the ability of some events

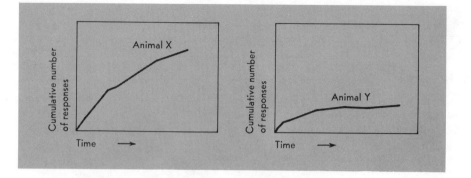

FIGURE 3-11. A comparison of the response rates of two rats pushing a lever for food.

to reduce tension. But it remained for Skinner and his students to produce an elegantly simple definition that not only sidestepped problems arising out of both of these earlier definitions, but also led to new insights. For Skinner, a reinforcement is any event that serves to increase the likelihood of occurrence of the response that produces it. Notice that, by this definition, the unconditioned stimulus used in Pavlovian conditioning is a reinforcer, as is the delivery of food in a Skinner box.

One immediate consequence of this definition is that reinforcers are always defined for specific animals in specific settings. While it may be possible to consider some events (e.g., the acquisition of food or water) as *usually* serving to reinforce behavior, there are obviously important conditions (e.g., after having eaten) under which they will not work.

Sometimes, under the right conditions, it is possible to increase bizarre behaviors by appropriate reinforcement. The importance of this fact is not in being able to produce bizarre behavior—Lord knows, the world has enough of that already—but in demonstrating the effects of reinforcement on behavior. Consider the case of "superstitious" behavior in pigeons. In order for "superstitious" behavior to be conditioned, you have to start with pigeons which have been kept hungry by feeding them a reduced diet so that they stay at 80 percent of normal body weight. In this condition, food serving as a reinforcement has a dramatic effect on whatever behavior it follows. In one of his experiments, Skinner placed hungry pigeons one at a time in a Skinner box and delivered reinforcements at *random* intervals *independent* of what the pigeon was doing.

A pigeon tended to seize upon and repeat over and over again whatever behavior it was doing just before reinforcement occurred. There is a good chance that this behavior would occur just about the time of the next random delivery of food and so would be reinforced again. This behavior soon comes to dominate the pigeon's activity.

Skinner likens the pigeon's "beliefs" to superstitious notions that people learn as a result of the chance joint occurrence of an act and a reinforcement. The primitive farmer does a dance and it rains. He dances again and again and again in the hope that this will bring rain once more. Occasionally this dance is followed by reinforcement. Under such conditions of reinforcement, it is difficult to extinguish the dance and the belief on which it is based. From now on the farmer may believe that in doing a dance he is able to bring on the rain. Plainly, reinforcement is an influential and powerful event.

Since reinforcement is so effective in controlling behavior, it should be possible to use it therapeutically to teach new behaviors to help a suffering patient. Probably the most important principle is that of *response shaping*, which is defined as the process of rewarding responses that approximate a desired final response. For example, if an experimenter wanted a dog to go to a wall, he would make the animal hungry and then give him some food for every response that tended to bring the dog closer to the wall. Initially the experimenter would reinforce any tendency in the appropriate direction, later only definite responses in that direction. In this way an animal would tend to go to the wall in a series of steps that gradually approached the desired final response.

In a famous case study, Monty Wolf, Todd Risley, and Hayden Mees of the University of Washington shaped a severely disturbed and hospitalized boy named Dickey to wear eyeglasses. Dickey had to learn to wear special glasses because he had just had an operation to remove cataracts, and an ophthalmologist had predicted that if Dickey didn't start wearing glasses within six months he would become blind.

The shaping procedure used by Wolf, Risley, and Mees consisted of a number of different parts. In the first part Dickey was not fed at breakfast, and bits of food were used as reinforcers. This drastic step was taken because candy did not serve as a powerful enough reinforcer and because time was quite important in this case. The second step involved reinforcing Dickey (giving him bits of food) for handling and picking up empty glass frames that lay around the room. The third step consisted of reinforcing him for putting the glasses on; while the fourth step involved reinforcing him for keeping them on once they had been put on. Because Dickey had a great many other behavior problems, he had some difficulty in learning to wear ordinary glasses, so that Wolf and his co-workers designed a set of glasses which fit like a cap and did not slide off easily.

A cumulative response curve of Dickey's glass wearing is shown in

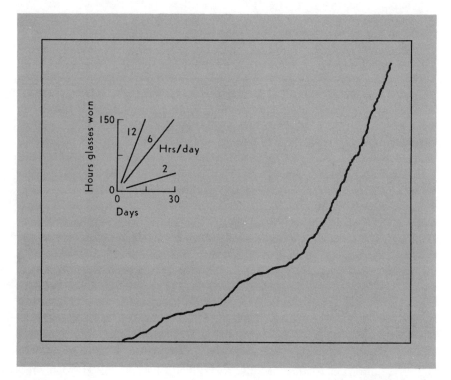

FIGURE 3–12.   Cumulative Record of Dickey's Glass Wearing. (From Wolf, Risley, and Mees, *Behaviour Research and Therapy* [Elmsford, N.Y.: Microfilms International Marketing Corp. (1964), p. 369. © 1964 *Pergamon Press Journal.*]

Figure 3–12. Although this curve doesn't directly show a simple event such as bar pressing, the steepness of the curve does indicate relative rate. From this figure it is obvious that Dickey ended up wearing his glasses for about twelve hours a day, from day 18 on.

SCHEDULES OF REINFORCEMENT

"The fisherman does not hook a fish with every cast of the line; the crop the farmer sows does not always yield a harvest." And the rat does not get a pellet every time he presses the lever—reinforcement does not always occur 100 percent of the time. The operant conditioner will often only reinforce once every other response, or once every ten responses, or even once every fifty responses. We use the term *partial reinforcement* to include such situations. When the partial reinforcement is regular (say, once every ten responses), we call it *ratio reinforcement.*

Interesting results occur when a partial reinforcement is keyed to time. *Interval reinforcement,* as this is called, does not depend on the number of responses made; an experimenter simply reinforces one response in a time period (for example, one response every minute). No matter how many responses are made, only the first one will be reinforced in any given one-minute period. These different *schedules of reinforcement* (100 percent; ratio; interval) each yield different and characteristic patterns of behavior.

Are these some typically human behaviors that depend on reinforcements of one kind or the other? Consider the victim of a partial-reinforcement schedule doled out by a "one-armed bandit" (gambling machine) at Las Vegas. Consider the workers who are paid a given amount of money for a given number of tons of coal dug or seams sewed. Consider . . . almost any and all human behaviors carefully, and you'll see the effects of reinforcement schedules on behavior.

EFFECTS OF PARTIAL REINFORCEMENT

In first training a subject to give a response, it is more efficient to supply a reinforcement with every response. Under partial reinforcement training is prolonged, but a response trained under this condition will continue long after reinforcement stops. A response trained under 100 percent reinforcement extinguishes quickly when reinforcement stops. The dramatic resistance to extinction exhibited by animals trained under partial reinforcement is shown in Figure 3–13. This figure shows the cumulative number of responses made by two groups of animals, one trained on a 100 percent schedule and the other on an interval schedule. The animals in both groups received two hundred reinforcements before extinction began. As is shown by the number of responses made before complete extinction occurred, the partially reinforced group was considerably more persistent than the 100 percent reinforcement group.

The practical importance of these results shouldn't be underestimated. For example, consider the case of child training. When we first teach a child to do something we should reinforce him liberally. As the child gains skill, reinforcement should taper off. By tapering off we assure the response a long life even when we are not nearby to apply frequent reinforcements.

In a larger sense, these observations are also important because they allow us to make contact with the world outside the laboratory. Although classical conditioning procedures can be extended to cover extra-laboratory situations, the fit is nowhere as smooth or as easy as is true of operant conditioning. It takes only a small number of observations to see reinforcement at work in almost any natural situation; and once you discover the reinforcing event, you are well on the way to controlling the behavior dependent on it.

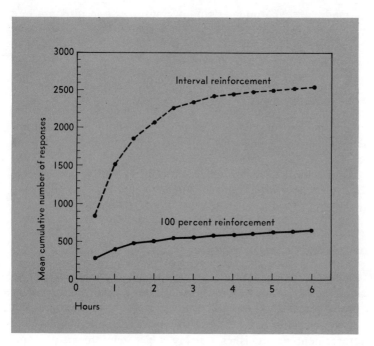

FIGURE 3–13. The effects of 100 percent reinforcement and interval reinforcement on the number of trials to extinction. [From W. O. Jenkins, H. McFann, and F. L. Clayton, *J. Comp. Physiol. Psychol.* 43 (1950): 158.]

A CASE STUDY OF RESEARCH IN
OPERANT CONTROL

If operant conditioning techniques can be used to control an organism's responses, Jasper Brener asked, would it be possible to control internal bodily processes such as heartrate on the basis of operant conditioning techniques? The advantage of such "behavioral" control of heartrate rather than the more usual drug control is that once the patient is taught how to control his own heartrate (or blood pressure or other internal response system), he needn't have drugs available to continue this control. In addition, drugs are not always effective in all cases.

In his early work Brener first determined the subject's normal heartrate in terms of its interbeat interval. If the interbeat interval was high, then heartrate was low; if the interbeat interval was low, then heartrate was high. Once the subject's normal interbeat interval was determined, Brener conditioned some subjects to slow down their heartrate (i.e., to increase their interbeat interval) and others to speed it up (decrease their interbeat interval). In order to do this, subjects had to produce an interbeat interval larger or smaller than two-thirds of the interbeat intervals they had previously produced or else they received a small electric shock.

Were subjects able to do this? Figure 3–14 shows the results for two subjects. In the left-hand graph we see results for a subject who was conditioned to decrease her heartrate (and did), while the right-hand graph shows the results for a subject who was conditioned to increase her heartrate (and did). The control subject in each experiment received exactly the same number of shocks as the experimental subject, except in the control case they were unrelated as to how fast or slow her heart was beating.

One important thing about this experiment is that it called into question the long-held assumption that only voluntary muscular responses could be conditioned on the basis of reinforcement procedures. Clearly, these results and others like them indicate that reinforcement can effectively come to exercise control over internal or autonomic responses.

Part of the reason psychologists previously assumed reinforcement didn't control autonomic responses directly had to do with the fact that

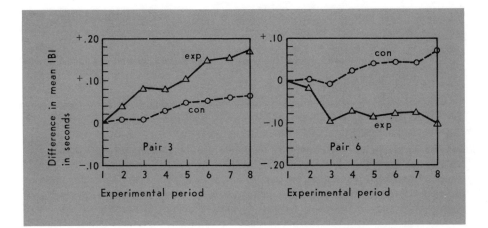

FIGURE 3–14. Changes in conditioned heart rate for two subjects. Note that an increase in the difference in the interbeat interval means the heart rate has been slowed (left panel), and a decrease means the heart rate has been speeded up. (From J. Brener, Heart rate as an avoidance response, *Psychol. Rec.* 16 (1966): 333.

those autonomic responses that are easiest to measure, such as heartrate, are known to be directly affected by muscular responses such as are involved in breathing. Under these conditions it is hard to be sure that subjects have in fact been conditioned autonomically rather than simply having learned to make muscular responses directly connected with heartrate or breathing, etc.

In order to do the proper experiment, Neal Miller and A. Banuazzi first injected rats with curare, a drug which paralyzes skeletal muscles but not internal organs such as the heart. The reinforcement used in one experiment involved electrical stimulation implanted in the brain of the type first described by Olds (See Chapter 1 for a more complete description). For some rats increases in heartrate were rewarded, while for other rats decreases were rewarded. The results of this experiment yielded exactly the same results for curarized rats as Brener had found for noncurarized humans: animals rewarded to decrease heartrate in fact slowed down, while those rewarded to increase it speeded up. These elegant experiments completely did away with the idea that classical and operant procedures operate on different response systems and further showed that autonomic functions can be directly altered by learning procedures.

This work has a great many significant implications. One that Miller has described is how a child might well learn psychosomatic symptoms on the basis of these procedures:

> For example, suppose a child is terror-stricken at the thought of going to school in the morning because he is completely unprepared for an important examination. The strong fear elicits a variety of fluctuating autonomic symptoms, such as a queasy stomach at one time and pallor and faintness at another; at this point his mother, who is particularly concerned about cardiovascular symptoms, says, "You are sick and must stay home." The child feels a great relief from fear, and this reward should reinforce the cardiovascular responses producing pallor and faintness. If such experiences are repeated frequently enough, the child, theoretically, should learn to respond with that kind of symptom. Similarly, another child whose mother ignored the vasomotor responses but was particularly concerned by signs of gastric distress would learn the latter type of symptom. I want to emphasize, however, that we need careful clinical research to determine how frequently, if at all, the social conditions sufficient for such theoretically possible learning of visceral symptoms actually occur. Since a given instrumental response can be reinforced by a considerable variety of rewards, and by one reward on one occasion and a different reward on another, the fact that glandular and visceral responses can be instrumentally learned opens up many new theoretical possibilities for the reinforcement of psychosomatic symptoms.

Simple Learning: A Summary and Comparison

We have considered the simplest type of learning under two broad head-ings: classical conditioning and operant conditioning. Let us summarize what we have said so far.

CLASSICAL CONDITIONING

Salivation in dogs and the knee jerk in human beings are responses that occur automatically, without training, if an adequate stimulus is presented. By pairing a neutral stimulus (the conditioned stimulus) with an adequate stimulus (the unconditioned stimulus), we can eventually make the response (conditioned response) occur to the previously neutral stimulus alone. This process is called *classical conditioning*. Further, the response will also occur to a stimulus similar to the conditioned stimulus; we call this *stimulus generalization*. We have shown how stimulus generalization may be useful in explaining more complex human behavior. If we continue to present the conditioned stimulus without the benefit of the unconditioned stimulus, we will soon *extinguish* the conditioned response—that is, it will no longer occur upon presentation of the conditioned stimulus. After a rest period, though, the conditioned response will *spontaneously recover* from the effects of extinction. We reported the following facts:

1. Conditioning is fastest if the conditioned stimulus precedes the unconditioned stimulus by half a second.

2. Though the process is difficult, it is possible to use a conditioned stimulus as an unconditioned stimulus for a new neutral stimulus in order to produce *higher-order conditioning*.

By making use of higher-order conditioning, it is possible to explain more complex learning on the basis of simple conditioning principles—for example, how the emotional meanings of words are learned.

OPERANT CONDITIONING

In operant conditioning a response typically occurs without any prompting by a specific stimulus imposed by the experimenter. If it is followed by an appropriate reinforcing event, the strength and likelihood of this response will increase. The nature of responses conditionable by reinforcement procedures is extremely broad: heartrate changes in human beings, bar presses in animals, key-pecking responses in pigeons, and so on. Just as in classical conditioning, a response in operant conditioning can be extinguished by lack of reinforcement. If in the original training, however, every response was not reinforced (a condition called *partial reinforcement*), extinction is delayed considerably.

You may have begun to wonder why we included separate discussions of classical and operant conditioning. They seem quite similar: both are forms of conditioning; if you withhold the reinforcement or unconditional stimulus, extinction occurs. Spontaneous recovery is a feature of both types of learning. In both we find stimulus generalization, discrimination, and higher-order conditioning. Indeed, the similarities are great.

What then, are the differences? Most of these are procedural in nature: in classical conditioning the occurrence of a conditioned response is *reflexively forced* by the unconditioned stimulus (salivation to meat powder, galvanic skin response to an electric shock); in operant conditioning the response is more voluntary (pressing a bar, uttering a statement of opinion). A related point is that in classical conditioning the unconditioned stimulus occurs without regard to the subject's behavior, whereas in operant conditioning the reward is contingent on the occurrence of a response.

To summarize the matter in functional terms: classical conditioning can be described as *preparatory* or *anticipatory*, whereas operant conditioning serves primarily to *emphasize* or *guide* an organism which already has certain critical responses available. All of these distinctions should be understood as simply representing relative emphasis. It is not easy to separate the two forms of learning completely. For example, it is virtually impossible to design an operant conditioning study that has no components of classical conditioning in it.

Complex Habits

THE LEARNING OF
SERIAL RESPONSE PATTERNS

chapter four

When an adult walks across a floor or reaches for an object, his actions appear to proceed in a smooth, uninterrupted stream. But slow-motion movies of these behaviors would reveal that they consist of many smaller ones. When you reach for something, for example, your arm is continually making slight adjustments in order to zero in on the desired object. This suggests that many sequential, or continuous, acts are composed of a string of smaller learned habits, as when a child spells a word or an adult ties his shoelaces.

In these and many other very ordinary cases, we see one fundamental property of behavior: the behavior occurs in time with one act following another. For this reason it is not surprising that psychologists have devoted a good deal of time and effort in trying to understand how people learn to perform sequential or serial acts. Many seemingly odd and irrelevant experimental procedures—such as having subjects learn nonsense syllables or master complicated mazes—have their roots in the psychologist's desire to learn how originally distinct responses come to form an integrated behavior chain.

SERIAL LEARNING

As a starting point, let us take a well-learned behavior sequence and analyze its characteristics. Reciting the alphabet is a good example. Most people can recite the alphabet rapidly and smoothly with few halts or errors; from the lips of a young child it is often an indistinct blur of sound of a few seconds' duration. When serial behavior is accomplished in this manner, we say that a *skill* has been acquired. Recite the alphabet backwards, however, and another property of serial behavior comes to light: its directional character. Even adults will require thirty to forty-five seconds to accomplish this task, often having to review parts of the alphabet in a forward direction before finding the next response.

Another point worth noting about this behavior is that it has a clear beginning and a clear end. Also, it seems as if each item in such a series is connected with all preceding items. In order to verify this impression, Benton J. Underwood and Rudolph W. Schulz conducted an experiment in which they asked subjects to respond with the first letter they could think of in reaction to letters of the alphabet. When subjects were asked to give their first response to the letter *f*, only 1.8 percent answered *g*; when they were asked to give their first letter association to the combination *e-f*, the proportion responding with *g* increased by a factor of 10 to 18 percent. When subjects were given the sequence *a-b-c-d-e-f*, the response *g* became a unanimous choice. In other words, as the string of letters was increased, the next item in the sequence became a more likely response. Since placing *a-b-c-d-e* before *f* increases the likelihood of the response *g*, Underwood and Schulz suggest the response *g* is at least partly determined by some small, remote S-R (stimulus-response) connections between it and each of the preceding letters.

Reviewing all of these factors, we can see there are three major aspects to any piece of skilled serial behavior:

1. It has a clear beginning and a clear end.
2. It has a definite direction.
3. Multiple connections often exist between any given response and those items preceding it in the series.

SEQUENTIAL HUMAN LEARNING:
EBBINGHAUS AND HIS LEGACY

The study of sequential human learning begins with Hermann Ebbinghaus. Although an experimental psychologist, Ebbinghaus was a student of philosophy and thus well acquainted with the idea of learning by contiguity—a concept which has been extremely influential in psychological theory. As was noted in Chapter 2, Pavlov's conditioning studies were received enthusiastically partly because they seemed to provide an experimental demonstration of the law of contiguity—i.e., that one response leads to another because they have occurred close together (in contiguity) in the past.

Ebbinghaus was very much aware of this principle, and when he decided to study how human beings learn serial orders he began by trying to find learning material that had never been experienced before. He needed such material because he did not want any previous connections between items to contaminate his results.

In 1885, Ebbinghaus published his remarkable experiments on memory for serial orders—remarkable in that Ebbinghaus was both the experimenter and the sole subject in the entire series. For a period of about twenty years, Ebbinghaus learned, relearned, and memorized lists of nonsense syllables. These syllables, which Ebbinghaus specifically invented for use in studying serial learning and retention, were simple to construct and handle and had no prior connections with other verbal materials. For his experiments, Ebbinghaus constructed about twenty-three hundred such nonsense syllables, writing out each consonant-vowel-consonant combination on a slip of paper. Before each experiment he shuffled the slips and drew out between twelve and eighteen slips. As soon as he had learned a particular list of nonsense syllables, he put them back into the pool, reshuffled, and drew out another set for the next experiment. In each experiment Ebbinghaus studied all syllables at the same time, and mastered each item in the list at his own rate. Consequently, he spent more time on some syllables (the more difficult ones) than on others.

Today, however, experimenters generally do not present such materials to subjects all at once, but rather in a device called a *memory drum* (see Figure 4–1). As the memory drum revolves forward in discrete steps the items to be studied appear one at a time in the aperture or window. The amount of time a subject can spend on each item is regulated. After the first presentation of the items, the subject's task is to anticipate, or state in advance, the next item on the list. The experimenter keeps track of the subject's hits and misses.

THE MAJOR PHENOMENA OF SERIAL LEARNING

Serial-position effect. Although Ebbinghaus established the major guidelines for work on serial learning and memory, it remained for later investigators to fill in many of the facts. One of the most complete early studies on the serial learning of nonsense syllables was done by Carl I.

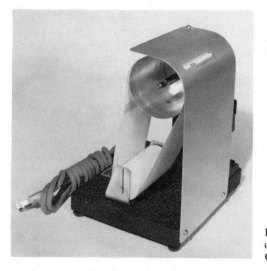

FIGURE 4–1. A simple memory drum. (Courtesy Ralph Gerbrands Co.)

Hovland of Yale University. Hovland had subjects learn a list of twelve nonsense syllables. He then counted the total number of errors that all subjects made at each of the twelve positions in the list. Hovland's results are presented in Figure 4–2, which shows that the greatest number of errors occurred in learning the syllable just past the middle of the series—a phenomenon called the *serial-position effect*.

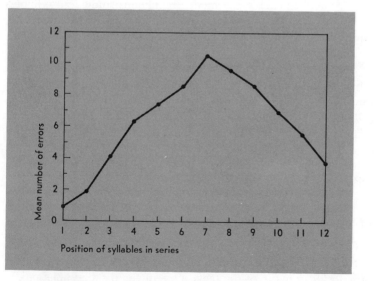

FIGURE 4–2. Mean number of errors made at different positions in a list of nonsense syllables. [From C. I. Hovland, *J. Exp. Psychol.* 23 (1938): 178.]

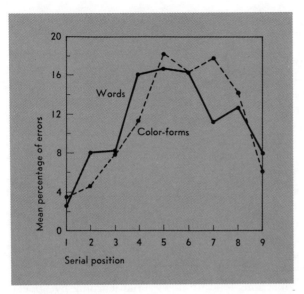

FIGURE 4–3. Comparison of the serial position effect for spelling errors and for learning a series of color forms. [From A. R. Jensen, *J. Educ. Psychol.* 53 (1962): 107.]

Spelling a word provides an interesting instance of serial learning. Arthur R. Jensen of the University of California compared the serial-position effect in learning to spell seven-, nine-, and eleven-letter words with the serial-position effect in learning a series of nine colored geometric shapes. Figure 4–3 shows the serial-position effect for both the nine-letter words and the nine-item list. The curves are quite similar. Jensen discarded the hypothesis that the spelling curve resulted from the ease of spelling prefixes and suffixes so that their presence in a word might artificially produce the serial-position effect. Through a careful examination of the data, he found that these elements elicited about the same number of errors as other parts of words. Furthermore, only a small proportion of the words he used had prefixes or suffixes.

Association in serial learning. When we pointed out earlier that the probability of *g* as a response to *f* increases when *f* is preceded by *a-b-c-d-e*, we referred to distant associations between each of these five letters and *g*. Such associations can also influence the errors made in the course of serial learning. A subject may fail to respond when asked to anticipate the next item in a sequence, or he may respond with an item out of sequence. Errors of the second type are either *anticipatory errors* or *backward errors*, depending on the direction they represent in the sequence. Anticipatory errors far exceed backward errors in number.

The occurrence of both types supports the notion that there are multiple connections among all the items in a serial list, whether these items are words, shapes, or nonsense syllables. Thus, words appearing early in the series may serve as partial stimuli for words appearing later in the list.

A more direct method of detecting these connections is to use an association procedure. In this procedure subjects first learn a list of nonsense syllables or words. At the end of training, they are presented with items from the original list and asked to say the first item each suggests. Most subjects tend to give the next item in the series as their first association. A few subjects initially give the item two places later, and fewer subjects give an item more than two places away. Figure 4–4 shows the number of associations in one such experiment for degrees of remoteness ranging from zero to eight items. Note that associations are less numerous in the backward than in the forward direction and that few associations are more remote than three items away.

To sum up: (1) connections exist between all items in a series; (2) these connections are stronger in the forward than in the backward direction; and (3) these connections tend to affect serial learning by appearing as anticipatory and backward errors. In order to learn the total serial behavior, these errors must be eliminated.

SERIAL LEARNING IN ANIMALS

One night in 1934, after the students had deserted the old psychology building at Yale University, psychologists assembled in a long hallway

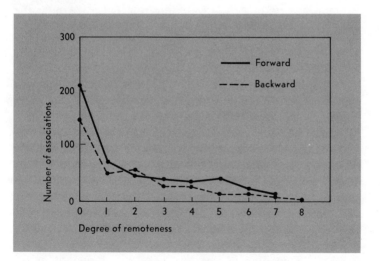

FIGURE 4–4. Number of forward and backward associations as a function of the remoteness between two nonsense syllables in a serial list. [From J. A. McGeoch, *Amer. J. Psychol.* 48 (1936): 221–245.]

to conduct an experiment with rats. They chose this particular corridor because they needed to string together seven narrow runways each 6 feet long, totaling 42 feet—far in excess of the length of their largest experimental room. Small boxes were placed at either end of the runway, one a start box and the other the goal box. Hungry rats placed in the start box then made their way down the runway to the goal box and food.

The hypothesis being tested was that the effect of a food reward would be greatest at the goal box and would decrease with distance away from it. Consequently, a rat's speed should increase as it moved down the runway. Each rat's progress across each section was timed and a curve (Figure 4–5) of its speed was plotted.

As Figure 4–5 shows, when approaching the goal box the rat's speed of running increased, reached a maximum just before the goal box, and slowed down a bit at the very end (because of the small size of the goal box—if a rat rushed into the goal box at top speed, it would likely crash nose-first into the end wall). This experiment demonstrated the general tendency for response speed to increase as an animal nears a goal. This tendency is called a *goal gradient*, referring to the fact that the effect of a reward diminishes with time and distance from the goal. The diminishing effectiveness of reward over time suggests that in training a child a small reward at the moment he performs a praiseworthy act will go a lot farther in strengthening that act than will a large reward much later.

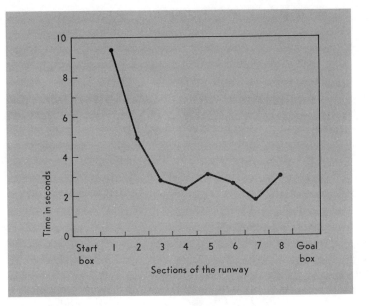

FIGURE 4–5. The goal gradient phenomenon in rats. This graph represents the amount of time in seconds it took a group of rats to cross each of the eight sections of a simple maze. [From C. L. Hull, *J. Comp. Psychol.* 17 (1934): 404.]

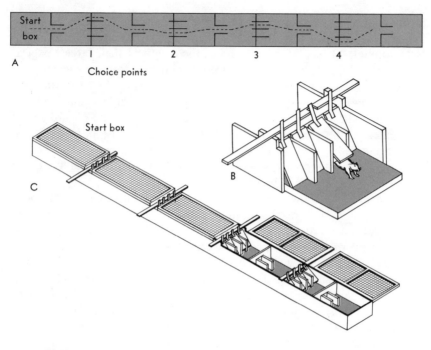

FIGURE 4–6. Straight maze used to study serial learning in rats. Part A shows the floor plan of one possible route through the maze; B presents a closeup of one set of doors; while C shows the overall nature of the maze. [From C. L. Hull and A. J. Sprow, *J. Exp. Psychol.* 37 (1947) 118–135.)

Investigators have also charted errors as a function of the part of the act in which they occur. The results of such studies have been quite consistent in research concerning both animals and humans. In work with animals, an apparatus similar to the one depicted in Figure 4–6 has been commonly used. The maze (shown in Part C) has a series of four separate sections. The entrance to each section is divided into four doors (see part B). In order to complete the maze, a rat is required to go through a different door in each of the four sections. The rat receives food only after completing the terminal section. Part A of Figure 4–6 shows one possible pattern a rat would have to learn in order to traverse the maze correctly. In this case the rat has to go through door 1 (counting from the animal's left) in section 1, door 3 in section 2, door 2 in section 3, and door 4 in section 4.

Did the seventy-two animals used in this study make a different number of errors at each of the four choice points? Figure 4–7 clearly shows that the number of errors differed at each of the choice points: most errors were made at points 2 and 3, the least at points 1 and 4. Here, then, is more evidence of differences in the ease of learning various com-

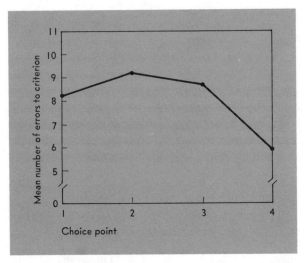

FIGURE 4–7. Number of errors made at four different choice points in a straight alley maze. [Adapted from G. A. Kimble, *Hilgard and Marquis' conditioning and learning* (New York: Appleton-Century-Crofts, 1961.)]

ponents of a serial task. For rats as well as for humans, items at the beginning and end of a series are easier to learn than those in the middle.

THE CHAINING HYPOTHESIS

One way in which to think about serial behavior is to consider it as a chain in which each separate response is a link. This straightforward assumption has a lot going for it; for example, any sequence can be thought of as a chain of S-R pairs in which neighboring responses are linked together because of the law of contiguity operating through the procedures of classical conditioning. The occurrence of anticipatory and perserverative errors suggests an additional assumption: each response is linked not only to its immediate neighbor but also to other responses some distance away. Thus if we have a list of five items—A, B, C, D, and E—the pattern of direct and remote connections would look something like the following:

In this figure immediate connections are indicated by a direct arrow, ⟶, while remote connections are indicated by a spanning arrow, ⟶. For each item A through E, the number of spanning connections have the following values: A = 0, B = 3, C = 4, D = 3, and

$E = 0$, where the values are obtained by counting the number of arrows that span each item.

Having described the *chaining hypothesis* in this way, we can interpret the major phenomena of serial learning as follows:

1. anticipatory errors (and by implication perservative errors) result from remote connections learned on the basis of conditioning; and

2. the serial-position effect results from having to inhibit spanning associates—i.e., since the greatest number of such connections span the middle item (item C), the learner is more likely to give an incorrect response here than at any other point.

Certainly this is a most ingenious and attractive hypothesis, and in fact for about twenty-five years was considered the correct explanation for almost all the major phenomena of serial learning. Unfortunately, one phenomenon never quite fit; so around the beginning of the 1960s psychologists, among them Sheldon Ebenholtz of the University of Wisconsin and Robert K. Young of the University of Texas, began to question the usefulness of a chaining hypothesis. The culprit-phenomenon causing most of the trouble had been described many years before by the German psychologist Helena Von Restorff (1933). In her experiment subjects were asked to learn a list of items in which one item was markedly different from all the others. For example, a subject might be asked to learn a list consisting of many words and one nonsense syllable. Contrary to what the chaining hypothesis would predict, subjects learned the nonsense syllable more quickly than any of the words, even if the nonsense syllable appeared in the middle (most difficult) position in the series.

A further and more recent series of studies by Eli Saltz and Slater Newman showed that having an isolated unit such as a nonsense syllable in the middle of a list did not speed up the overall rate at which the whole series was learned. However, the subject was made more aware of the different item and produced it as a correct response more often than a word identically placed in the same list. The most important part of the Von Restorff effect is that it forces us to consider reference points in learning. This means that, at least in the Von Restorff case, a learner may use the isolated item as a point of reference and learn the rest of the list in relation to this point.

But even serial orders with no specific Von Restorff item have two very obvious reference points around which to build learning—the beginning and the end. If we extend the Von Restorff argument a bit, we see that both the beginning and end of a serial order can serve as reference points from which all serial learning might proceed. If this is true, subjects having learned a list of items should be able to name the first and last items more readily than the sixth, seventh, or tenth item in a sixteen-item list.

Rudolph W. Schulz tested this prediction in 1955, and results were as expected; subjects had no trouble telling the experimenter the first and last items but had much trouble placing items in the middle of the series. In addition, a more recent study by Arthur Jensen has shown that the order of learning a ten-item list in terms of item position is 1, 2, 10, 3, 9, 4, 8, 5, 7, and finally 6. This order obviously gives rise to the familiar serial-position effect.

But more compelling evidence against a simple chaining hypothesis is supplied in a study by Sheldon Ebenholtz. Ebenholtz argued that if the beginning and the end of a list serve as significant reference points, then changing the beginning item on each trial should make it extremely difficult for subjects to organize their learning. It would take longer, Ebenholtz argued, to learn the same series of words if the list began with a different item on each trial than if it began with the same item, even if everything else remained the same. The results of such an experiment showed that it took almost one-and-a-half times as long to learn a series with no clear beginning or end than one that always started and ended at the same place (i.e., twenty-two trials as opposed to thirty-five trials).

Another strong piece of evidence against a simple chaining hypothesis was supplied in a series of studies by Robert K. Young. Young reasoned that if, in learning a serial list such as *boy, July, aid, ticket, letter*, chained connections were in fact established between neighboring items, subjects who had learned the list should then be able to learn the following list of four pairs almost at once.

boy—July
July—aid
aid—ticket
ticket—letter

Several different studies have been done by Young and other experimenters testing exactly this prediction; in almost all cases, subjects who first learned a relevant serial list learned a second list of pairs no faster than subjects who first learned an irrelevant list. Although these data do not conclusively rule out chains, they do weaken the chaining hypothesis considerably.

But all of these results are destructive; they do not tell us what the subject *is* doing as he tries to learn a series. In order to be more constructive and descriptive, it is necessary to consider a different approach to the problem of serial learning. One such approach was initiated by

Clinton DeSoto and J. J. Bosley of Johns Hopkins University and carried out more extensively by Howard R. Pollio and his associates at the University of Tennessee.

The DeSoto-Bosley procedure is a simple one: the subject is asked to learn to pair up groups of boys' names (or other items, such as girls' names or nonsense syllables) with different response words. In the original study twenty-eight college students, evenly divided according to college class, had to learn to associate each of sixteen names printed on cards with the label *freshman, sophomore, junior,* or *senior*—that is, four boys' names for each class label. During testing, each subject was shown the cards one by one and then had three seconds to supply the label; he could then check the back of the card to see whether he had been right or wrong. After each presentation, the set of sixteen cards was shuffled by the experimenter and the procedure repeated. Note that in this procedure there is no serial order on any trial; the only serial order is that which the subject carries around with him (in his head) from previous learning—in this case, the order of class year. Nevertheless, the results of this experiment showed that all twenty-eight subjects made an average of 7.9 errors in learning pairs involving *freshman* as the response word; 10.4 in learning *sophomore* as the response word; 9.1 in learning *junior* as the response word; and 8.9 in learning *senior* as the response word. In short, the usual serial-position effect appeared despite the fact that the only serial order on any given trial was the one the subject brought to the experiment on the basis of prior learning.

These same results have been found to apply when response terms were items like the numbers 1, 2, 3, 4, and 5 or the words *beautiful, pretty, fair, homely,* and *ugly* or the words *hot, warm, mild, cool,* and *cold.* In the latter two cases (using words), the subjects almost certainly had never learned to use the response words in that order before (even though it does make sense to organize them in such a sequence). Since the serial-position effect occurs so regularly, Ebenholtz has assumed that the only prerequisite for producing a serial-position effect is some ordered series of items, regardless of whether or not these items had ever been learned or used in that order before.

One unexpected finding emerged from the study in which the *hot . . . cold* series was used: subjects did not produce a serial-position curve during the winter and summer months, whereas they did produce such a curve during the *spring* (see Figure 4-8). In the summer months subjects learned pairs involving *hot* most easily, whereas they learned pairs involving *cold* most easily in the winter. These results further support the idea that subjects search for anchor points and build their learning around these points: what could be a more natural anchor point than the word *cold* in winter and the word *hot* in summer?

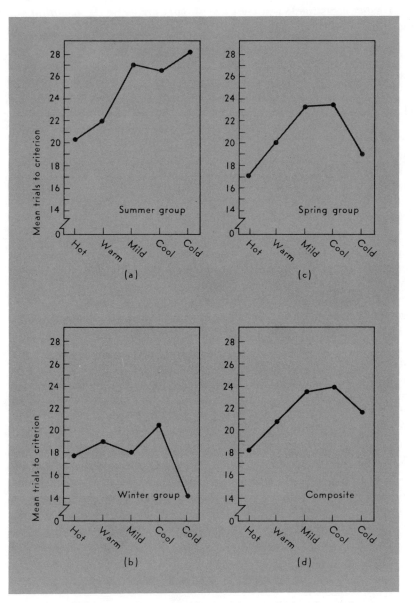

FIGURE 4–8. Mean number of trials to criterion for each response term as a function of season. (From Pollio, Deitchman, and Richards, *J. Exp. Psychol.* 79 (1969): 209.

One other result of these experiments deserving of comment concerns the errors subjects made as they learned pairs involving the *beautiful . . . ugly* series. If we look at the number of times a subject said *pretty* or *fair* when the correct response was *beautiful*, we can measure something like remote connections in the context of this experiment—that is, if we consider saying *pretty* when *beautiful* is correct as a 1-degree remote error, saying *fair* when *beautiful* is correct as a 2-degree remote error, and so on for *homely* and *ugly*, we can draw a curve showing the relationship of number of anticipatory errors to distance between items. Such a curve would be comparable to the curve of remote associations (see Figure 4–4) found in serial learning. When such curves have been drawn for the DeSoto-Bosley case, they produce results very similar to those found in serial learning of the nonsense-syllable type—that is, a smaller number of errors as the distance increases. This was true despite the fact that there is a very strong tendency for *beautiful* to produce *ugly* as a response in free-association tests. These results lead us to suspect that serial learning may also involve item-to-item connections and that these connections are particularly obvious in the middle of the list.

All in all, this last result (that errors decrease as distance increases) suggests that we needn't throw away the chaining hypothesis altogether; all we really have to do is supplement it with the idea of reference points. At this point, the best summary we can offer concerning what goes on in serial learning is as follows: the beginning and end of a series are learned most readily because they are most easily noticed by subjects. This in turn allows the subject to use these positions as the primary cues in learning a series. However, position is a very poor cue in the middle of a series, and for this reason the subject must resort to an item-by-item chain. Such chains grow toward the center of the series from the natural anchors provided at both ends.

Although this seems a reasonable hypothesis at present, there is no reason, or even hope, to believe that it will go unchallenged for as long as did Ebbinghaus's original chaining hypothesis. There is undoubtedly a measure of truth in both a chaining and a reference-point hypothesis, for both seem to be involved in what happens as a subject learns a serial order of responses.

Motivation and Learning

chapter five

When Julie Andrews performs in front of an audience of more than three thousand people at Carnegie Hall, she is not only very good, she is even better than when she practiced by herself before the performance. When twelve-year-old Ricky Fishman plays the piano by himself he makes no mistakes; when he plays before fifty or so friendly people in his school auditorium, he hits the wrong chord six times. Why does Julie Andrews get better under the pressure of an audience, and why does poor Ricky Fishman get worse?

Perhaps the most important thing about these observations is that Julie Andrews has been singing for years and singing represents a very "simple" task for her. On the other hand, Ricky has been playing the piano for only four months and for this reason he still finds it an extremely difficult and demanding task. What all of this seems to mean is that the performance of a well-learned (really, an overlearned) skill is improved by being put under pressure, and that the performance of a poorly learned skill is overwhelmed by being put under similar or even less pressure.

THE YERKES-DODSON LAW

Since singing is such a "simple" task for Julie Andrews and piano playing is still such a difficult one for Ricky, the anxiety produced by performing in front of an audience seems to facilitate performance in Julie's case and to hinder performance in Ricky's. The tendency for high levels of motivational arousal (such as high anxiety) to facilitate very skilled performances and to disrupt not very skilled ones forms the basis of a psychological law described over sixty years ago by R. M. Yerkes and J. D. Dodson, and called, in their honor, the Yerkes-Dodson law.

This law was derived from some experiments done in 1908. In these experiments, mice were taught to discriminate between two stimuli that differed in brightness. When they made a mistake during learning, they were given an electric shock, the intensity of which was high for some mice and low for others. The results of these experiments showed that high levels of motivational arousal (high shock intensity, in this case) facilitated learning of an easy discrimination but hindered the learning of a difficult one (in this case, where stimuli were very close to each other in brightness).

In a more recent test of this law in 1957 by P. L. Broadhurst, rats were trained to swim through a Y-shaped maze submerged under water; when a rat reached the fork of the Y, it had to choose between one door which was brightly lit, leading out of the water, and a second, locked, door which was poorly lit. The decision of which fork to choose was least difficult for rats when the illumination of the doors was sharply contrasted, moderately difficult when the doors were closer in brightness, and most difficult when they were equally illuminated. To induce motivation ranging from moderate to high, Broadhurst submerged his rats for 0, 2, 4, or 8 seconds in water *before* permitting them to swim toward the doors, thus there were three levels of task difficulty and four levels of motivation. Learning was measured by observing the number of correct choices a rat made when it arrived at the fork of the Y.

Figure 5–1, which presents the results of this experiment, supports the Yerkes-Dodson law—i.e., as task difficulty increases, the optimal anxiety level for performance decreases. When the rats could easily discriminate between the doors, longer submersion (higher motivation) facilitated performance. The difficult task was best facilitated by the smallest amount of anxiety, but any increase in anxiety led to drastic deterioration in performance.

In addition to the "Julie Andrews–Ricky Fishman–swimming rats phenomenon," the Yerkes-Dodson law has also been found to apply to

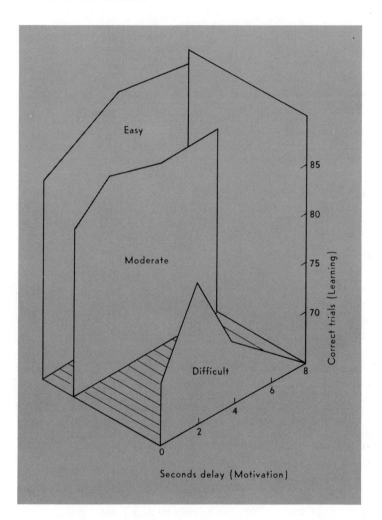

FIGURE 5–1. A three-dimensional model illustrating the Yerkes-Dodson law. Rats were deprived of air by restraining them under water for a varying number of seconds and were then permitted to escape by selecting the correct door. Optimum motivation for learning depended on the difficulty of the choice task. [After P. L. Broadhurst, Emotionality and the Yerkes-Dodson Law, *J. Exp. Psychol.* 54 (1957): 345–352.]

how well students do on tests—that is, very anxious students perform well on easy test questions and very poorly on difficult ones. In summary, then, strong motivational states, such as anxiety, or need for air, or level of electric shock, etc., facilitate learning up to a point, the location of this point being determined by the difficulty of the task.

DEFINING MOTIVATIONAL EVENTS

In studying the effects of motivational states on learning and performance, we must recognize that what we take to be evidence of motivation is always inferred from what some organism is doing, has done, or isn't doing. When we talk about relating motivation to learning, the term *motivation* is usually used to describe some hypothetical or arbitrary state within the organism—such as, for example, anxiety, hunger, or thirst. Such states are usually assumed to arouse an organism to some activity. Depending on which psychologist one is reading, such arousal may simply "activate," "energize," or "drive" an organism in some nonspecific way; or, again depending on the particular psychologist, such arousal may also serve to "guide" or "direct" an organism to some goal as well. Regardless of which view is taken, motivation is always an inference from behavior, and in order to make this inference we need to examine some of the specific things that specific organisms do at rather specific times.

One tell-tale sign used to infer the operation of one or another motivational event occurs when the same stimulus conditions produce different responses at different times for either the same person or for many different people. For example, if we give a child a candy bar on Monday and he eats it, smiles, and says "Thank you," but on Tuesday he throws the candy on the floor, we may feel justified in saying that his motives must have been different on each day. Perhaps on Monday he was hungry and on Tuesday he wasn't; or perhaps on Tuesday he was angry at you and on Monday he wasn't. In either case, we infer the operation of one or another motivational event from the fact that the child's behavior changed in the absence of any clear change in the situation itself.

In a similar way, we infer a motivational state when a sleepy infant suddenly wakes up and begins to cry: he may not have been fed for four hours and he's "hungry"; or he hasn't been played with for a while, and is therefore "bored"; or . . . who knows what. Similarly, we will surely infer a motivational event of some kind or other if a female rat is observed to run about nine miles in a squirrel cage on a particular day in contrast to a usual daily run of less than a mile. If we also discover that she again runs a mile a day after being spayed, we may feel reasonably sure that the motivation for her nine-mile run was probably sexual in origin. As a matter of fact, if we examine the total course of activity in a normal female rat, we will find that her running increases periodically, and that this period of increased general activity is related both to her sexual hormonal cycle and to her receptivity to male rats. With this further data, we may feel even more justified in assuming the operation of sexual motivation in bringing about heightened general activity in the female rat.

There are other tell-tale signs that have been used to infer the operation and existence of motivational events. A partial list of these is given by Judson Brown in his book *The Motivation of Behavior* (1961):

1. *Variability of behavior in the presence of constant stimulus conditions.* This situation is of course represented by the cases already described—that is, where the young child takes the candy on Monday but never on Tuesday, or where the rat runs nine miles on Wednesday, but "never on Sunday."

2. *Extremely strong responses brought about by very weak stimuli.* The creaking of a set of stairs in a deserted house will evoke strong reactions of escape in a timid explorer; the weak cries of a sick infant will propel its mother into action; and the odor of a female dog in heat will arouse a male dog to excited activity. In all cases, the response seems disproportionately large given the extremely weak nature of the instigating event.

3. *Constancy of behavior in the presence of a changing environment.* The captain who stays with his ship even when the ship is in danger of sinking presents a case where we would want to introduce motivational concepts— such as, perhaps, the need to succeed, or fear of failure—to describe his actions in any sensible sort of way.

All in all, Brown has provided a reasonable set of situations in which it seems appropriate to infer the operation of a motivational event or events. In any case, the important thing to remember is that motivation is always an inference from behavior, and that the value of assuming motivational events rests in whether or not it serves to explain phenomena which are difficult, if not impossible, to explain otherwise.

The Measurement of Motivation

Since motivation, like learning, is always an inference from performance, psychologists have had to be quite ingenious in devising different ways to measure motivation. One simple way is to measure the general-activity level of an organism; another is to measure the rate at which an organism performs some act it has learned in the past. A slightly different technique is to measure the number of obstacles an animal will overcome in order to reach one or another goal.

MEASURING GENERAL-ACTIVITY LEVEL

Drive, as the energizing factor of motives (or motivation) is called, often refers to a physiological condition (such as hunger or thirst) defined in terms of how long an organism has been deprived (of food or water, for example) The strength of a primary drive of the kind brought about by food deprivation has been correlated to an organism's level of activity as measured by using an activity wheel, a circular cage that rotates freely around its axis. (The typical apparatus contains a wheel, which is near a small area in which the animal eats and sleeps, and a counter which records the revolutions of the wheel as the animal runs in it.)

It seems that an increase in drive will lead to an increase in activity— up to a point, that is. So, for example, the length of time a rat is deprived of food should be roughly proportional to how much running around the cage it does. Similarly, increasing sexual drive (e.g., by deprivation or by hormonal variation) should be reflected in how much activity an animal will engage in. G. H. Wang found this to be true in a study of female rats housed in an activity-wheel apparatus. In female rats, the *estrus cycle* (cycle of sexual receptivity) is between four and five days; in other words, every fourth or fifth day the adult female rat is sexually receptive or sexually motivated. Wang measured activity level and found that activity hits its maximum near the peak of sexual receptivity. The

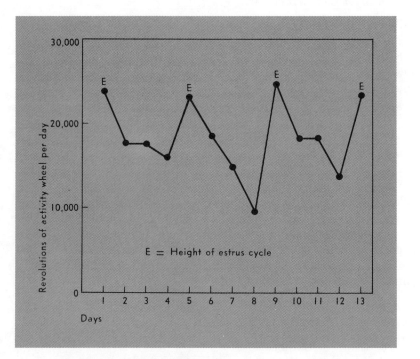

FIGURE 5–2. Activity and the estrus cycle. The period of greatest activity corresponds to the period of sexual receptivity. [After Wang, 1923.]

periods of low activity correspond to unreceptive periods. Figure 5–2 shows how the general-activity level varies over different parts of the complete cycle.

RATE OF ACTIVITY

The hungrier a rat is, the greater its drive and the faster it will press a bar in an apparatus that releases food. Speed of bar pressing can therefore be used as an indication of drive level in rats. W. T. Heron and B. F. Skinner trained a number of rats to press a bar in a Skinner box to obtain food pellets, all the while permitting them to eat their fill, and then starved them for many days. Next their daily diet was restricted to food pellets obtained by pressing the bar in the Skinner box. The amount of food received in this way was too little to sustain life. Each day, following a four-minute period, the food-delivery mechanism was shut off and the rats remained in the box for an additional hour. The increasing effect of hunger was assessed by daily changes in the number of bar-pressing responses made during this hour. This measure reached a peak on the fifth day (see Figure 5–3) and then decreased rapidly as the rats began to suffer the physically debilitating effects of starvation. It seems clear that up to a point, responsiveness increases with increases in primary drive.

Drive, also an important concept in human learning, has been described by Janet Taylor Spence in terms of anxiety level. Spence reason-

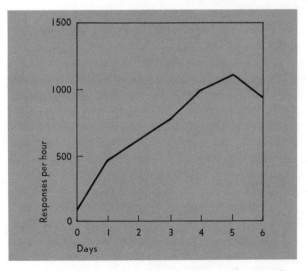

FIGURE 5–3. Change in the mean number of responses per hour made by thirteen rats during six days of food deprivation. [From W. T. Heron and B. F. Skinner, *Psychol. Rec.* 1 (1937): 51–60.]

ably hypothesized that, in some situations, the more anxious a person is the more rapidly he would respond. First she developed a self-report test to be called a "Manifest Anxiety Scale" based on items which a majority (at least 80 percent) of clinical psychologists polled considered to describe manifest symptoms of anxiety—including "yes" or "no" questions such as "I worry more than other people," "I sweat easily even on cool days," etc. Then, using tested individuals, she ran experiments in learning a simple conditioned eyelid response. Assuming that, in a simple situation, higher drive would produce superior performance and that anxiety heightens drive, Spence expected highly anxious individuals to learn the response faster than those who were less anxious. Her expectations were confirmed: subjects with high scores on the Manifest Anxiety Scale exhibited more vigorous eyelid conditioning early in the conditioning session (see Figure 5–4).

This result is consistent with the Yerkes-Dodson law, for the conditioned eyelid response is a simple response, and simple responses are facilitated by high levels of arousal. Therefore, we would expect that the

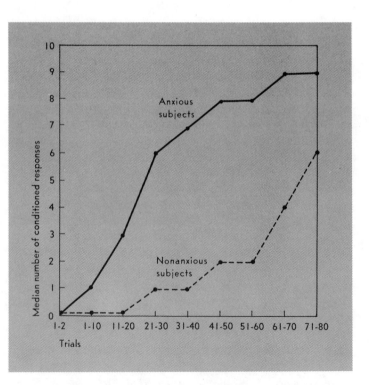

FIGURE 5–4. The effects of high and low anxiety on the speed of learning a classically conditioned eyelid response. [From J. A. Taylor, *J. Exp. Psychol.* 41 (1951): 88.]

more anxious a person, the faster he would learn this simple task. In support of the Yerkes-Dodson law, Spence and others have also found that high levels of anxiety as measured by the Manifest Anxiety Scale interfere with more difficult tasks, such as problem solving or complicated concept learning.

OVERCOMING OBSTACLES

How much shock will a hungry rat endure? Some forty years ago, C. J. Warden conducted an experiment in which he placed a hungry rat in a start box and permitted it to run across a grid to a goal box filled with food. After several such trials, Warden charged the grid with electricity, thus giving the rat a very strong shock while crossing it. A record was kept of the number of crossings the rat made within a twenty-minute period, along with the amount of shock the rat was willing to endure, giving us some measure of the strength of his drive to reach the goal box. The drive was found to be strongest after four days of food deprivation (see Figure 5–5).

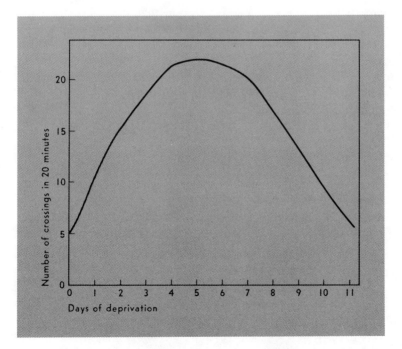

FIGURE 5–5. Each day a rat had to cross an electrified grid in order to obtain food. The number of times the rat crossed in twenty minutes is shown as a function of the number of days it was deprived. [After C. J. Warden, *Animal Motivation* (New York: Columbia University Press, 1931).]

Worth noting here is the difference between *drive* and *need*. Rats starved for eight days certainly have a greater *need* for food than rats starved for four days. But the rat deprived for eight days does not necessarily have a stronger *drive*, since it may be considerably weakened by lack of strength; thus, although people on a hunger strike may report their subjective feelings of hunger as being cyclical (sometimes stronger, then weaker, and then stronger), their need for food is steadily increasing regardless of how it seems to them.

Types of Motives

PHYSIOLOGICAL MOTIVES

The motives which are physiological in nature are the same as those constituting primary drive—e.g., food, water, air, sex, pain avoidance. These motives are based on actual bodily needs and are not learned, unlike a motive such as the desire for sportscars.

Broadhurst's experiment with oxygen-deprived rats mentioned earlier is an example of an animal-learning experiment in which a physiological drive or motive was manipulated. We saw in that experiment that rats performed an easy task best at high levels of deprivation, whereas for the most difficult task optimal performance occurred at a lower level of deprivation.

Charles Cofer and Mortimer Appley (*Motivation: Theory and Research*, New York: Wiley, 1964) have summarized the effects of manipulating physiological drives on learning: when you deprive an animal of food, his speed of responding is usually faster; if you deprive him of air, or if you apply some other aversive stimulation, his correct responses tend to increase, up to a point, and then to decline. In general, the Yerkes-Dodson law tells us that the point at which they start to decline is related to task difficulty.

ACQUIRED MOTIVES

Money in the bank: how it acquired value. In an experiment by J. T. Cowles, chimpanzees were taught to work in return for poker chips that could be used later to get grapes from a "chimp-o-mat" (a vending machine for chimpanzees—see Figure 5–6). As soon as the chimps had learned that the poker chips could be traded in for grapes, they would work just as hard for chips as they would for grapes. Sometimes they would save up several chips before cashing them in for grapes. (Rather than saving the chips in a savings bank or under the mattress,

FIGURE 5–6. The poker chips that can be used to obtain food have acquired incentive value. [From Hilgard, Atkinson, and Atkinson, *Introduction to psychology* (New York: Harcourt Brace Jovanovich, 1971) 310.]

the chimps usually just clutched them or placed them in a pile in the corner.) Although the chimps worked fastest when the chips could be immediately cashed in for grapes, they were also able to postpone gratification, even completing fairly complex tasks, before claiming their primary reward.

The importance of this experiment is that something other than a primary reward has acquired value—in this case the poker chips because they could be used to obtain food. The way in which the chips acquired incentive value for the chimpanzees probably mirrors the way in which dimes and quarters and dollar bills have acquired incentive value for many humans. Just as the chimpanzees learned that their chips could be used to "buy" grapes, so we have learned that dimes and dollars can be used to buy things that will satisfy primary motives. Acquired motives, such as the motive to work for money or chips, are motives which are learned.

Fear: a learned motive. Just as it is possible to teach chimps to value originally neutral objects such as poker chips, so too it is possible to teach rats to become afraid of an originally neutral room. Once they acquire this fear, they will do anything and everything to avoid that room.

The original experiments on this topic were done by Neal Miller at Yale. Miller placed rats in a box with two compartments, one white with a grid floor and the other black (see Figure 5–7). The rats were at first indifferent to this treatment. Their indifference was drastically modified by shocking them ten times in the white compartment. Each time the shock came, they were allowed to escape into the black compartment. Later, when placed in the white compartment without being given any shock at all, they ran quickly into the black one.

Miller then closed the door between the compartments. Now the rats could escape from the white compartment only by learning to turn a drum that opened the door. When placed back in the white compartment the rats showed the usual signs of extreme fear or anxiety—urination, defecation, and crouching. Eventually, they moved about and accidentally turned the drum opening the door. When this happened they ran into the black compartment.

Just as the rats were becoming efficient at turning the drum, Miller made the drum inoperative. No amount of drum turning would budge that door; instead, a lever press was substituted to open the door. At

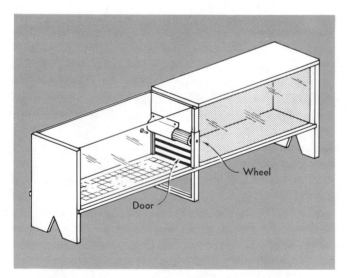

FIGURE 5–7. Apparatus used to train fear. Compartment A is painted white, compartment B black. Electric shocks may be given in compartment A. Under different conditions the door (painted with black and white stripes) may be removed, and a low hurdle put in its place. [Adapted from N. E. Miller, Learnable drives and rewards, in S. S. Stevens (ed.), *Handbook of experimental psychology* (New York: Wiley, 1951.)]

first the rats showed the same signs of extreme fear as before, but eventually they stopped trying to turn the drum and learned to press the lever. All of this behavior was motivated by the fear originally learned in response to the cues of the white compartment. Miller's classic experiment demonstrates how rats learned to acquire fear as a motive in itself: it was learned through its association with pain. The reason we can now think of fear as a drive is because it will motivate the learning of new responses.

In another experiment, Miller taught rats to strike each other in order to terminate a highly aversive electric shock. If there was no other rat in the cage to strike, a single rat would "displace" this learned aggressive response onto a doll present in the cage. If there was neither another rat nor a doll in the cage, a single rat would strike the walls of the cage. What does this experiment show? Driven by the motive of fear, a rat will transfer or displace his aggressive response from one stimulus (another rat) to another stimulus (a doll or wall). People displace aggressive responses too. If your father hit you and you failed to hit him back (say, because of fear of the consequences), you might instead hit your younger brother, or yell at your best friend.

MORE COMPLEX MOTIVES

There are several strong motives other then the acquired ones discussed above that do not seem to be based on specific physiological needs. These are found in very young organisms in many different species. The two that seem of greatest generality are: (1) the manipulation motive, and (2) the need for stimulus change.

The manipulation motive. In 1881, a monkey belonging to G. Romanes spent two hours trying to open the lock of a trunk which had nuts inside. The monkey didn't particularly need the nuts since there was a pile of them nearby. The three-month-old son of Jean Piaget, the great Swiss psychologist, once spent fifteen minutes shaking a rattle suspended above his crib. Since rattle shaking and lock manipulating apparently do not satisfy physiological needs, the only reward to be gained from these behaviors seems to be the sheer fun of the activity. Indeed, monkeys and babies both like to manipulate new objects. The fact that monkeys will play for hours with a mechanical device placed in their cages, will take it apart and put it together and take it apart again—without any evident reward whatsoever—has led Harry F. Harlow to postulate that monkeys —and other animals as well—have a motive for manipulation that is just as basic as any other animal motive (see Figure 5–8).

Harlow's assumption of a "manipulative motive" is just one example

FIGURE 5–8. The monkey takes the latches apart, even though there is no "incentive" or "reward" except that deriving from the manipulation itself. [From Harlow, Harlow, and Meyer, 1950.]

of the attempt to deemphasize the idea that all motivation states somehow depend for their effectiveness on drive reduction, such as occurs in the reduction of hunger and thirst. Other psychologists have also stressed such positive motives as the needs for exploration, organization, achievement, and so on. Their work suggests that the opportunity to explore and manipulate the environment can serve as a powerful motivating force.

Motivating agents such as these are called *competence motives*, mainly because their expression increases the ability of an organism (human or otherwise) to deal competently and effectively with its environment. The next section deals with one rather specific and rather important aspect of competence motivation: the need for stimulus change.

Need for stimulus change.   At McGill University twenty-two male college students were given twenty dollars for every twenty-four hours they would spend lying relatively motionless in a soundproof room on a foam rubber bed, wearing translucent goggles, gloves, cardboard cuffs around their arms, and with a U-shaped foam rubber pillow for their heads (see Figure 5–9). No activity was required of them; in five days, though, they could earn a hundred dollars. Yet few of them were able to stand

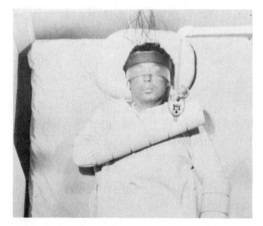

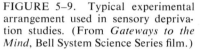

FIGURE 5–9. Typical experimental arrangement used in sensory deprivation studies. (From *Gateways to the Mind*, Bell System Science Series film.)

the experience for more than two or three days. The students found it exceptionally difficult to sleep or think; they had hallucinations and became panicky; and they dealt poorly with intelligence tests introduced during their stay in the room. When they emerged from the experiment they were often disoriented, confused, nauseated, and fatigued for periods up to twenty-four hours. While some of these effects may have been due to the suggestibility of the subjects, the root of this disorder of behavior seems to be a need for stimulus change.

Perhaps the capacity to be bored is one of man's important qualities, though we share this capacity with lower animals. Rats and monkeys, at least, have shown a need for changing stimulation which can motivate new learning. In one experiment Robert A. Butler and Harry F. Harlow showed that monkeys who were not hungry or otherwise deprived would learn to differentiate between panels of different colors with no other reward than the opportunity to look through a window into another room. In another experiment rats were trained to distinguish between the white and black arms of a T-maze. The only reward for a correct choice was the opportunity to explore a more intricate maze for one minute. The mean number of correct choices in the T-maze showed a significant increase as the number of trials increased. Rats chose the side that provided the greater stimulus change.

The results of all these and other experiments indicate that both men and animals respond favorably to changes in stimuli. Everyone gets tired of things that they have too much of. People who eat lots of hamburgers often get tired of hamburgers and crave a piece of pizza. People get tired of listening to Beethoven and start to listen to more Bach. This "getting-tired" process is called *habituation*. Presenting a familiar stimulus over and over results in boredom, and sometimes even strong aversion. If we do get bored with a stimulus and the stimulus is then withheld for a period of time, the stimulus may recover to its original level of interest. After a month of no hamburgers, we may get to like them again.

What does all this have to do with learning? This desire for a change in stimulus conditions is often strong enough to induce the *learning* of new responses that will bring about changes. The experiment by Butler and Harlow is an excellent example of how animals learn a new response that will only serve to bring about a change in the stimulus environment.

If "boringness" of a stimulus condition leads to a tendency to avoid that condition, then the effectiveness of novelty in evoking new behavior should diminish as an animal becomes more familiar with a new situation. In support of this supposition, a number of studies have shown that although rats tend to explore new objects, this tendency diminishes as the animals become more familiar with the objects. Due to stimulus generalization, other objects similar to the now-familiar ones will also be ignored. This result is perfectly congruent with the others we have mentioned and would suggest that the slogan "It's time for a change" applies to stimulus conditions as well as to politicians.

Does Motivation Affect Learning or Performance?

In Chapter 1 we saw what happened when a rat, well educated in a T-maze, had eaten his fill: he slept. We pointed out at that time that this shows that performance depends, in part, on motivation. In order for a rat to perform well, it must not only have learned where in the T-maze the goal box is located, but it must be motivated to run to the goal box.

In this section we shall consider the question of whether motivational level affects learning or performance, or both. To explore this question experimentally we must train subjects under different levels of drive (say, one hour and twenty-two hours of hunger) and then test to see whether *learning* differences have resulted. One difficulty is that, during testing, the subject *must* be under some level of hunger. If he is fully fed before testing (zero hunger), then the *test* condition will be more like the one-hour than the twenty-two-hour *training* condition. A decrement in response might result for the animals trained under twenty-two hours of food deprivation simply because of the change in internal stimuli. Testing under twenty-two hours of food deprivation would distort the test results of the one-hour group.

A study by Donald J. Lewis and John W. Cotton made use of a special research design to overcome this problem. Two groups of rats were trained to run in a straight alley maze under one and twenty-two hours of drive respectively. The day after training, one-half of each group was tested after one hour of food deprivation and the other half after twenty-two hours. Testing consisted of seeing how many trials it took to extinguish the running response. Presumably, if it took longer to extinguish, it must have been a more thoroughly learned habit. The results are presented in Table 2. The numbers in the table report the average number of trials it took to extinguish the running response.

Note that there are two *row* totals (207 and 220) and two *column* totals (175 and 252). Each column total is contributed to by rats *trained* under one hour of deprivation and an equal number of rats *trained* under twenty-two hours of deprivation. The contribution of the training drive, therefore, is equal for each *column* total. The difference in column totals thus reflects performance differences brought about by the differences in drive magnitude during extinction. As we might expect, during extinction the higher drive (twenty-two hours) resulted in more responses before extinction was complete. Similarly, each row total is equally influenced by the drive during extinction. Drive during extinction, then, would not be responsible for any difference in the row totals. The only condition that might have produced such a difference is drive during training. If drive during training did produce a difference in behavior during extinction, this would be the kind of relatively permanent change in behavior we ascribe to learning. In this experiment the row totals do differ. The higher drive for the twenty-two-hour group during learning was carried over to the testing (extinction) stage. The effect is small, but it is still there. Evidence of the same effect in other (although not all) studies suggests that learning under higher drive leads to somewhat greater resistance to extinction.

Before we jump to the conclusion that we learn better under higher drive, let us examine another consideration. Several experiments have shown that during such experiments the high-drive group seems to leave the starting box more quickly than the low-drive group, and that once learning has begun, the high-drive group traverses the maze in

Table 2

Number of Trials to Extinction as a Function of Hours of Deprivation in Acquisition and Extinction

| | | HOURS OF DEPRIVATION IN EXTINCTION | | TOTAL |
		1	22	
Hours of Deprivation in Acquisition	1	90	117	207
	22	85	135	220
	Total	175	252	427

SOURCE: *Learning and performance as a function of drive strength during acquisition and extinction* (J. Comp. Physiol., 1957, *50*, 189–194).

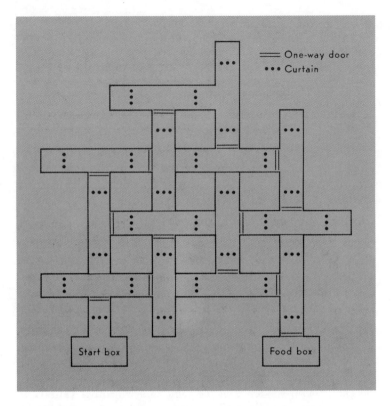

FIGURE 5–10. Diagram of maze used in latent-learning experiment. [After E. C. Tolman and C. H. Honzik, Insight in rats, *U. of Calif. Pub. in Psych.*, 4(1930): 14. Reprinted by permission of The Regents of the University of California.]

quite a businesslike manner, while the low-drive group is a bit more meandering and exploratory. Both groups may in fact be learning equally well, but one group has learned the habit of making steady progress, while the other has learned the habit of making slow, uneven progress. These considerations suggest that differences in drive are likely to produce qualitative difference in learning; that is, animals learn slightly different responses, rather than different degrees of the same response. Also, when we restrict ourselves to evaluating performance in such rigid terms as number of trials to criterion, we run the risk of losing important insights into the processes under investigation.

LATENT LEARNING

If not all measures are equally good in helping us find out what's going on in a particular experiment, it is also entirely possible that a par-

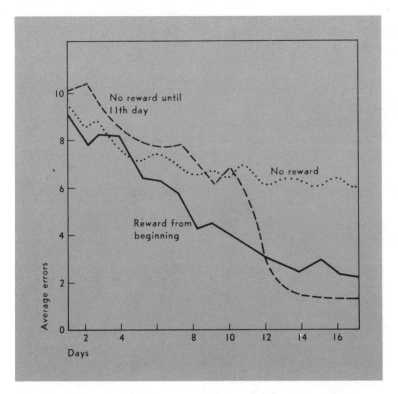

FIGURE 5–11. When rats who had not been rewarded for ten days finally receive food rewards, they perform slightly *better* than rats who had been rewarded all along. [After Tolman and Honzik, 1930.]

ticular performance does not always reflect all that we have learned or know. Learning that does not always show up under all conditions of performance has been called *latent learning*, and was studied most extensively by E. C. Tolman and C. H. Honzik. In one of their early experiments, three groups of rats were run every day in a very complicated maze (see Figure 5–10). The first group got a food reward from the goal box at the end of the maze. The second group were simply allowed to explore the maze; when they arrived at the goal box, there was no food reward, and the rats were removed from the maze. The third group was allowed to explore without a food reward for the first ten days and received a food reward in the goal box for the last seven days. The number of errors in reaching the goal box that each group made on each day is shown in Figure 5–11, which shows that the number of errors decreased across days for all three groups, meaning that all groups must have learned something. Notice that the group rewarded with food from the beginning made fewer errors than the other two groups. But the really striking thing about these results is that the errors made by the third group dropped drastically as soon as they started receiving food rewards—so drastically that by the twelfth day they were making fewer errors than the group that was rewarded all along. What this means is that before rats in this third group got any reward at all, they had learned something about the arrangement of the maze. In Tolman's terms, they had formed a "cognitive map" of the areas they had explored.

On the basis of this study, we may postulate that learning and performance can be distinguished experimentally. Clearly, learning went on in the absence of reward, but only when reward was provided were we able to see the effects of what had been learned.

The Learning of Concepts
and the Transfer of Learning

chapter six

If you've ever been a nine-year-old, then you probably remember with great fondness collecting the cards that came in bubble-gum packages—the kind with pictures of athletes, movie monsters, rock groups, or whatever on the front and some biographical information on the back. Printed on the back of a baseball player's card, for example, would be his team, his age and other vital statistics, his batting and fielding averages, and so on. (See Figure 6–1.)

But do you remember what you used to do with such cards? First—keeping baseball cards as our example—you probably sorted them into leagues and then into teams. But since that's fairly obvious and not very challenging, you might have then picked one aspect, such as batting average, and then ordered the cards in each team on that basis. However, in that case you would find that you had mostly outfielders and thus in order to arrive at the best possible hitting team you would have to pick players on the basis of two factors: their position *and* their batting average.

If you paid attention to how well they fielded and wanted to pick the best fielding team, again you would have to select players on a combined basis—in terms of their fielding average *and* the position they played. If

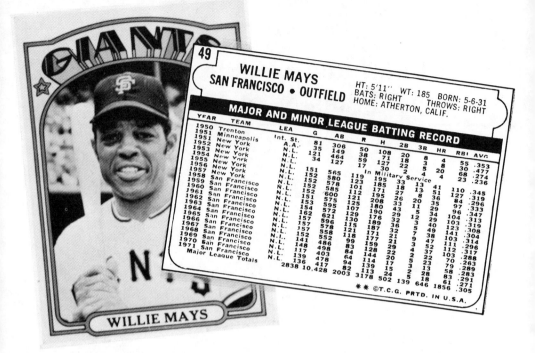

FIGURE 6–1. Baseball card. (This card from the private collection of David Pollio and Frank Derby, Knoxville, Tenn.)

you wanted the best fielding and hitting team, you would have to use a threefold classification: position *and* batting average *and* fielding average. There are undoubtedly many other ways in which you could have ordered your cards: most home runs hit, best pitching percentage, age, color, weight, place of birth, and any and all combinations of these and other factors. The possibilities are almost infinite; and if you've ever watched a nine-year-old at work on his baseball cards, you know that he can spend all of the rainy days in a year organizing and reorganizing these cards.

But did you ever realize the psychological significance of such behavior? Children engaged in this kind of activity are actually putting things into concept-based categories. In the language of the learning laboratory, each card (i.e., each player) is an example of some *concept*; and each concept can be described on the basis of a number of *factors*, *dimensions*, or *attributes* (these three words are often used synonymously). Let's take a few of these attributes and see how it is possible to represent any given baseball player in terms of the pattern he produces for some set of attributes.

ATTRIBUTE

NAME	Batting Average	Fielding Average	Age	Weight	Position
Willie Mays	.301	.982	40	185	Center field
Pete Rose	.302	.964	29	194	Left field
Lou Brock	.287	.978	32	170	Right field
Hank Aaron	.314	.958	37	180	First base

Once we consider players in this way, there are a number of different things we can do with the set of attributes defining each player. Considering concepts in this way—Willie Mays = [.301, .982, 40, 185, CF] In more formal terms, Willie Mays is a *concept exemplar*, and all of the values contained within the brackets are his *vector* or *list* or *set of attributes*.

When we consider each player as a list of attributes, we can do lots of other things in the way of concept studies; for example, we can ask which two of the four players described above are most similar. In terms of our present way of looking at things, we should compare each attribute of each ballplayer with those of each of the other players; the two whose differences are least would be the most similar. So, for example, in terms of age Mays is most similar to Aaron, and in terms of batting average Mays is least similar to Brock. In this way, the similarity of two concepts can be defined and given a precise numerical value.

Now that we've got all this data, what can we do with it? We can see that not all attributes are equally important for all concepts. If you wanted to fill out the concept of the ten best hitters, only one attribute would be relevant: batting average. This is a *single-valued concept*, and whether the ball player is a third baseman or a good fielder or weighs 185 pounds or fits any other attribute is irrelevant. All that matters is his batting average.

But sometimes we need to take into account more than a single attribute, as when we want to field a regular nine-man team with the best combined batting average. In this case two attributes are important, batting average *and* position played. How would we go about doing this? We would first order all our cards on the basis of position played and then pick the best batter for each position. This type of concept—one that depends upon the joint contribution of two attributes—is called a *conjunctive concept*. There are many other types of concepts, but these two illustrate the points that concepts can be defined in terms of their constituent attributes and that many different possibilities and combinations exist, even for a limited set of items such as baseball cards.

FROM BASEBALL CARDS TO CONCEPT
LEARNING: PROCEDURES AND STRATEGIES

In all of the cases described so far, the formation of a concept always begins with some kid sorting his bubble-gum cards. In most experiments on concept learning, however, it is the experimenter who selects the concept and the subject who must discover what it is. There are two main ways in which such an experiment can be conveniently conducted: by using either a *reception* procedure or a *selection* procedure. In a typical *reception procedure* a subject is presented with a series of cards, the first of which is the concept exemplar; he then must tell the experimenter, by answering "yes" or no," whether each subsequent card is also an example of the concept.

A typical series, once again involving our baseball cards, might start off as follows:

CARD NO.	PLAYER	ATTRIBUTES	CORRECT ANSWER
1	Willie Mays	Outfielder—yes; home-run hitter—yes; Met—yes; black —yes . . .	Yes
2	Carl Yastrimski	Outfielder—yes; home-run hitter—yes; Met—no; black —no . . .	Yes
3	Johnny Bench	Outfielder—no; home-run hitter—yes; Met—no; black —no . . .	No
4	Lou Brock	Outfielder—yes; . . .	Yes

The experimenter's concept here is *outfielder*, although there are other possibilities he could have used, such as home-run hitter, black, etc.

Bruner, Goodenow, and Austin (1956), after examining the records of many different subjects, described two different strategies college students use in solving problems of these types: a *wholist strategy* and a *partist strategy*. When he uses the wholist strategy, the subject tries to remember as many of the attributes of the concept exemplar as he can and compares those attributes with those of the second card. The subject then proceeds to the third card, remembering the attributes of the first card with a kind of footnote provided by the second card—thus, in our example, after viewing the Yastrimski card the subject would conclude that all of Willie Mays's attributes are relevant to this task except his team, his color, etc. . . . . The third card makes these footnotes more precise, and the fourth card is used as a test to confirm the concept as: *Willie Mays → outfielder.*

A subject using the *partist strategy* focuses on one attribute at a time; for example, after viewing the first card he may guess that the concept is "Met," or "home-run hitter," or "outfielder." He then sees if each succeeding card confirms or denies his supposition. If the subject picks the correct attribute, he will learn the concept quickly; if not, he may never learn it. For this reason, most subjects studied by Bruner, Goodenow, and Austin learned the greatest number of concepts by using the wholist rather than the partist strategy. In general, the wholist strategy is much more effective, largely because its flexibility allows the subject to alter his conjectures as he goes along.

In a typical *selection procedure* a number of cards—for example, ten or twenty bubble-gum cards—are laid out in front of the subject, and the experimenter shows the subject another card—for example, the Willie Mays card—that exemplifies his concept. The subject must then pick out cards, one at a time, that he thinks illustrate the experimenter's concept. After each selection the experimenter tells the subject whether his choice was correct.

How do subjects learn concepts in this type of procedure? Bruner and his coworkers describe two basic approaches: focusing and scanning. Thus, in our example, once the subject had been shown the Willie Mays card as the concept exemplar, he might approach the problem of picking out the next card by first *focusing* on as many attributes of Willie Mays as he could keep in mind. For instance, he might focus on the attributes "outfielder," "home-run hitter," "black," and "Met," and then pick another card that varied not at all, or in only one way. If the subject picked Hank Aaron and the experimenter said, "Yes, Aaron is a positive example," then the subject could eliminate "Met" as a relevant attribute. If the subject next picked Yastrimski and the answer were again "yes," he would then know that both "black" and "Met" are irrelevant. By the subject's selection of cards, an experimenter can infer which attributes the subject is paying attention to and, therefore, which strategy the subject is using. As this example indicates, the focusing strategy is analogous to the wholist strategy used in a reception-procedure experiment.

Subjects using the *scanning* strategy start out by assuming that many or most of the concept exemplar's attributes belong to the concept; in other words, they make a hypothesis of the following form: the concept is a *black, home-run hitting outfielder* who plays for the *Mets*. Once this is done, the subject continues to select other players who match this total pattern—e.g., Tommy Agee—until his hypothesis no longer works, and then switches to a different total hypothesis and starts picking out cards all over again. This strategy is usually much less successful than a focusing strategy, mainly because it requires the subject to remember all previously tested and rejected hypotheses.

Using either strategy, most subjects, as soon as they think they have guessed the concept, tend to pick cards that would confirm their hypothesis. Such cards are called *positive instances of a concept*, as opposed to *negative instances* (cards which do not illustrate the concept). Many studies have shown that subjects generally find positive instances much more natural to use in learning concepts than negative instances. This is probably the case because our educational system works on the assumption that it is better to teach someone "what a concept is" rather than "what it is not." If this tendency to use only positive instances is learned, it should be possible with appropriate training to teach subjects to use negative instances.

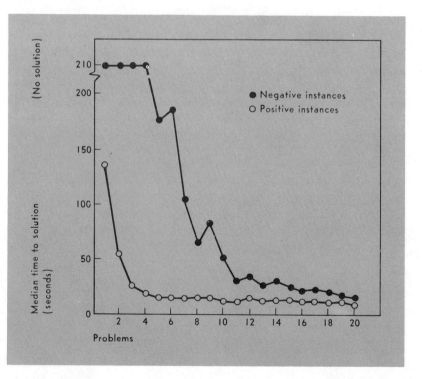

FIGURE 6–2. Median time to solution of twenty consecutive problems for subjects working with only positive or only negative instances. [Data from Freibergs and Tulving, *Canad. J. Psychol.* 15 (1961): 103.]

In the early 1960s Freibergs and Tulving performed the following experiment to determine whether subjects could learn to use negative instances: two groups of subjects were given twenty consecutive concept problems. One group was shown only positive instances, while a second group was shown only negative instances; both were then asked to describe the concept. Figure 6–2, which presents the results for both groups, shows that although subjects using only negative instances were unable to solve any of the first four problems, by the fifteenth problem there were only small differences between their proficiency and that of the group using positive instances. In a sense, then, it is possible to learn to use negative information in solving concept problems, and as we shall later see, this sort of increasing proficiency in learning to solve problems of a particular type is significant to the topic of problem solving in general.

Once this important point has been clarified, let us see if we can go back and come to some conclusion as to how experimental procedures and subject strategies are related in concept-learning studies. Bruner, Goodenow, and Austin (1956) have discussed the major difference between reception and selection procedures. "In the reception procedure, the subject's major area of freedom is in the hypothesis he chooses to adopt. . . . In the selection procedure, it is in the manner in which he chooses instances to test." Both procedures occur in real-life situations, and any attempt to understand concept learning must take these differences in procedures and strategies into account.

ATTRIBUTE IDENTIFICATION AND CONCEPT LEARNING

Certain concepts are easier to learn than others, particularly in the laboratory. Why? In very early work on this topic, Edna Heidbreder hypothesized that ease of learning depends on the kind of concept involved—specifically, that concepts representing concrete objects (trees, faces, hats) can be learned more easily than more abstract concepts that cannot be represented by a single picture (such as threeness or justice). In an experiment in which subjects were asked to learn concept "names" for pictures of the sort in Figure 6–3, Heidbreder confirmed her hypothesis: subjects learned, for example, to respond with the correct "name" for the different kinds of faces before they learned to respond with the correct "name" for the various pictures containing three objects.

H. D. Baum, however, challenged Heidbreder's interpretation. Repeating Heidbreder's experiment, Baum noted that subjects frequently experienced confusion and that most confusion occurred with pictures that could elicit competing concept "names." Thus, if twoness was repre-

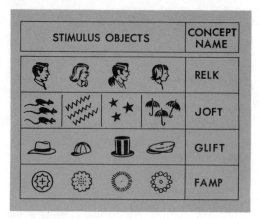

STIMULUS OBJECTS	CONCEPT NAME
	RELK
	JOFT
	GLIFT
	FAMP

FIGURE 6–3. Types of stimuli used by Heidbreder in her study of the development of concepts. Notice that although each of the stimuli differs from the others, the four stimuli that carry a common name have a basis of similarity. [From E. Heidbreder, *J. Gener. Psychol.* 24 (1946): 93–128. Adapted by D. D. Wickens and D. R. Meyer, *Psychology*, rev. ed. (New York: Holt, 1961), p. 362.]

sented by two faces, subjects often responded with the "name" that had been assigned to "faceness." Abstract concepts are almost always represented by instances in which many other competing concept attributes are embedded, which is not so often the case with examples of concrete concepts like "trees." Such competing responses can make concept learning quite difficult, as when a child is learning to apply the concept "building" to both a shack and a skyscraper.

This analysis of concept learning in terms of competing responses suggests that knowing some or all of the attributes that an individual assigns to [or associates with] each stimulus in a group of stimuli would enable us to know of any competing responses to the stimuli, and therefore would allow us to predict the ease or difficulty the individual would experience in concept learning. Benton J. Underwood has proposed a theory of concept formation that is relevant here. He suggests that learning or recognizing concepts requires that one see relationships among stimuli; in order to see such a relationship, it is necessary that the same attribute be suggested by each member of a group of stimuli. For example, if a child sees a blue triangle and a blue square, he must think of the attribute "blue" with regard to both stimuli before he can see the relationship and form that concept. To understand that a group of animals are dogs, a child must have learned to label them appropriately and must have the response "dog" to each member of the group.

Underwood and Jack Richardson prepared a set of verbal materials which made it possible to conduct research along these lines. They asked undergraduates to produce *sense impression* word associations to each of a large group of words. This meant that when a word was shown, the subject had to give the first word he thought of that mentioned color, shape, size, texture, smell, or some other sense impression. Underwood and Richardson succeeded in finding groups of words which had an associate in common. For instance, the words *atom, crumb, flea,* and *gnat* all elicit the associate *small.* In fact, small was the sensory associate to *atom* in 87 percent of the cases, to *crumb* in 79 percent, to *flea* in 86 percent, and to *gnat* in 76 percent of the cases.

A good deal of research has been conducted using these materials. As might be predicted, it has been found that the greater the average probability of the stimulus-concept association in a group of stimuli, the faster the concept is attained. Consider, for example, the following four words:

Baseball   Head   Button   Knob

What sensory-impression concept do these words represent? No doubt you very quickly came up with "round." You might have also responded "hard." But you more than likely came up with "round" first, because as a sensory associate to these four words, "round" has a tested average probability of 66.25 percent, whereas "hard" has a probability of only 8.25 percent.

If we take another group of four words, however, we can reverse the situation:

Knuckle   Hailstone   Skull   Stone

What sensory-impression concept do these four words suggest? In this case, "hard" is the most likely response (with a tested average associative probability of 52.5 percent); "round" is considerably less likely, with an average associative probability of 11.25 percent.

Underwood and Richardson have shown that the probability of a particular concept association being made is an extremely powerful factor in determining ease of concept attainment. In these terms we can now look back at the Heidbreder materials in Figure 6–3 and understand better the relative difficulty in attaining the abstract concept. The concept "threeness" is not a highly likely response to the picture of three mice; the description "hat," however, is an extremely dominant response to pictures of hats. In short, concept learning is strongly affected by the dominance of the relevant attribute, particularly when extremely complicated exemplars are used.

TRANSFER OF LEARNING

Concepts give generality to our experience. If it were not for concept formation and concept usage, we would have to respond to each concept exemplar as if we knew nothing about it and would have to learn its meaning in each new situation. Concepts are essential for transferring knowledge or skills gained in one situation to another situation. If you had to learn how to drive every new car you encountered, there could never be an Avis or a Hertz.

For this reason it is not at all surprising that most early discussions of transfer of learning concerned school learning. There is no point in a child learning how to do something only *in school*; what matters is how well the child can transfer his school learning to the world outside school. Learning that stays specific to the school is likely to produce an unsuccessful child or adult (unless, cynics may claim, he happens to be a teacher).

This early work on transfer of school learning revolved around the old controversy of whether it is better to teach specific skills—the identical-elements theory—or general skills—the formal-discipline theory. Most early schools operated on the latter theory, which assumes that the mind is like a general, all-purpose muscle and that intellectual exercise of the kind provided by the study of Latin and mathematics strengthens the mental muscle better than the learning of manual skills.

The formal-discipline theory was severely attacked in a number of ways by the great American psychologist Edward L. Thorndike. In one study done in 1924, Thorndike administered IQ tests to about eleven hundred high school students who comprised two groups—those who studied academic subjects such as Latin and mathematics and those who studied manual-training subjects such as typing and cooking. After one year the students in both groups were again administered IQ tests. In addition, the students were given achievement tests in both academic and manual-training subjects at the end of the year.

The results were quite clear: the academic group scored seven points higher than the manual-training group on this second IQ test. On the face of it, formal-discipline theory seemed indicated—if it were not for the fact that the academic group had scored seven points higher on the first tests (taken the year before) as well. In short, there was no change in the relative position of the groups. Of more importance for Thorndike, however, was the finding that manual-training students scored higher on manual-training achievement tests and academic students scored higher on academic achievement tests. Although this is no surprise, it does indicate that the effects of training are a lot more specific than is required by the formal-discipline theory.

On the basis of these and the results of other studies, Thorndike and his coworkers became convinced that transfer only occurs between two different tasks to the degree that the tasks involve identical or similar elements. Once the problem is stated in this way, it opens up the door for an analysis of transfer based on an S-R analysis of tasks. That is, transfer can now be studied in terms of the degree of similarity of stimulus and response requirements between two tasks.

Such an approach is obviously quite congenial to laboratory experimentation, and for this reason the theory of identical elements gave a very strong push to an analysis of transfer in terms of stimulus and response factors.

Stimulus Factors in Transfer.   In Chapter 3 we considered one type of transfer based on stimulus factors, *stimulus generalization*, in which a response transferred positively from one situation to the next because of the similarity of the situations. When the same response is required in two such similar situations, the amount of positive transfer to be expected from the old situation A to the current situation B can be described as shown in Figure 6–4: as the current stimulus situation becomes less and less similar to the old situation, the amount of positive transfer decreases.

Response Factors in Transfer.   According to a respected rule of thumb in psychology, when you move from one situation to another you will always get negative transfer if you keep stimuli constant but change the responses. A good example of this is a person who has learned to drive a car using a clutch and then switches to the same model car with automatic transmission. The stimuli are not too different, but the responses will change radically. This individual will find himself stabbing frantically for the clutch with his left foot and fumbling around with his right hand in the place where the gearshift should be. In the laboratory,

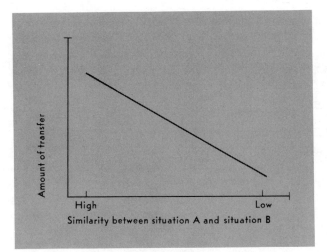

FIGURE 6–4. Hypothetical curves showing transfer on the basis of similarity between situations.

learning the pair *xad-piv* will be harder if you have previously learned *xad-gej* than if you have learned a pair without *xad* in it.

One subtle example of how compatibility of responses makes positive transfer possible can be seen in a study by Jarvis Bastian. Bastian first had subjects learn a list of nonsense syllable–word pairs, like *xad-dark*. Then he divided the pairs into three groups that were differentiated by substitutes for *dark*; the substitute responses were *light, black,* and *calm*. For example, now a subject might learn *xad-light*. Bastian found that the substitution of the first two words (light or black) produced marked positive transfer. The reasons are not difficult to find. First, the words *light* and *black* are closely related to the word *dark*; indeed, 829 of 1,008 college students gave *light* as their first association to *dark*. Second, the responses are not incompatible. Subjects can easily *think* the word *dark* between the stimulus and new response without interfering with their performance; thus,

$$xad \rightarrow (dark) \rightarrow light$$

In this experiment we see exceptions to the general rule that replacing a response with a new response produces negative transfer. When the two responses involved are compatible, positive transfer is possible. This clearly suggests that, when responses are replaced, one reason for negative transfer may be incompatibility between responses—i.e., the old interferes with the new.

SUMMARY OF S-R PRINCIPLES

If we consider a task as consisting of a specific stimulus and response pair (S_1–R_1), it is possible to examine what happens as we vary one or both of these components. If we hold both the stimulus and response items constant, we expect maximum positive transfer. In this condition we are only giving our subject one more learning trial. If we hold the response term constant but vary the stimulus term, we expect some positive transfer, the exact amount depending on the similarity between S_1 and S_2. If we hold the stimulus term constant but vary the response, we expect negative transfer in most cases. Only if R_1 and R_2 are not incompatible would we expect some slight positive transfer. Although we can exercise control over stimuli and responses in the laboratory, it is difficult to find situations in which only the stimuli vary or only the responses change. A baseball player learning golf, a one-wall handballer learning four-wall handball, and a college student learning his second foreign language are examples of transfer situations that defy simple analysis in terms of either stimulus or response. In most such cases where we vary *both* the stimulus and the response term, we expect some negative transfer.

LEARNING HOW TO LEARN

We all know individuals who can solve difficult puzzles and tricky problems in a fraction of the time it takes most of us. Much of their facility is doubtless due to their being attracted to such pastimes and, consequently, having practiced many puzzles before. But their facility extends even to puzzles in which the stimuli and responses could not bear any direct relationship to puzzles they have seen before. Here we have a situation of positive transfer where both stimulus and response factors have changed. Often such positive transfer can be ascribed to *learning how to learn*, that is, learning a mode of attack.

Probably the best evidence of the mechanisms involved in learning how to learn comes from a series of experiments by Harry F. Harlow and his associates at the University of Wisconsin. In Harlow's experiments a monkey was given a series of discrimination tests using two wooden blocks. In each test the blocks were different in terms of some obvious visual cue—one would be white, the other black; one cylindrical, the other conical; one striped, the other plain; and so on. Some reward, such as a raisin, was placed in a well under one of the blocks, and the monkey was allowed to look under only one block in each trial in a test series. If on his first test trial the monkey lifted the white block and did not find the raisin, he would be using optimal strategy if on the second trial he looked under the black block. For the first few tests with different pairs of blocks, the monkey did no better than chance on both the first and second trials. As the monkey gained more experience in the test series, his second guess in any specific test series became consistently better. In fact, after most monkeys had done about two hundred different cue-discrimination tasks, they chose the correct block about 90 percent of the time on the second trial. After mastering three hundred discrimination problems, the monkeys were 95 percent correct on their second trials.

Furthermore, the monkeys seemed to learn general habits in response to the total test situation. For one thing, they learned which aspects of the situation were important and which irrelevant; for example, they learned to respond to the pattern rather than to the position of the block. Finally, they learned to *change* their responses: after a number of tests, if the prize was not under the first pattern selected, they tried the other pattern on the next trial. If we only observed these monkeys being tested on their three-hundredth problem, we might be tempted to ascribe their

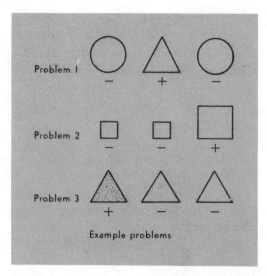

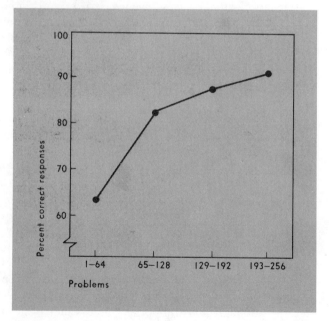

FIGURE 6–5. (Top) Three sample oddity problems. The subject is rewarded on each trial only if he chooses or responds to the odd member, marked +, of each stimulus set.

(Bottom) Actual data from a study of oddity learning in monkeys. (Moon and Harlow, 1955) The score plotted on the ordinate is the percentage of responses to the odd stimulus on trial 1 of each problem. After 250 problems these subjects make about 90% correct trial 1 responses. [From Lyle Bourne, *Human Conceptual Problems* (Boston: Allyn and Bacon), p. 16.]

performance to "insight." Knowing their previous experience, however, gives us an understanding of what factors brought about this "insightful" behavior. It also suggests the role of learning how to learn in our daily lives. We continually encounter new situations to which we must respond adaptively. These new situations are usually similar in form to things we have experienced before. Learning to learn efficiently enables us to show what we call insight, rather than random, trial-and-error behavior.

Such learning-to-learn effects can also be observed when children or monkeys are required to learn a complex concept such as "the odd one in a set of three." Obviously, it is very difficult to talk about stimulus and response factors when the stimulus and response change with each trial. Harlow's monkeys did these problems as follows. In Figure 6–5, the general form of the task is presented in the top panel. The monkey is rewarded only if he chooses the stimulus marked by a "+." How the monkeys performed in this task is shown by the graph in the bottom panel, which shows a general learning curve for successive problems. By about the two-hundredth trial, the monkeys were solving about 90 percent of the problems presented to them. As can be seen, on the first problem monkeys made about 50 percent errors, whereas they made almost no errors by the two-hundred-fiftieth problem, at which point we can say that concept learning is complete because transfer is unfailing.

Similar learning-to-learn results have been found with rats running mazes and humans learning lists of nonsense syllables. In both cases it takes longer to learn the first maze or the first list in a series than it does to learn subsequent ones. In the case of nonsense-syllable studies, learning how to learn involves a number of different factors. If a memory drum is being used, subjects must learn the rhythm of the device. In paired-associate learning, individuals learn to bridge the pairs with a mediating word—i.e., nonsense syllables are examined for their resemblance to real words. In addition, many irrelevant responses drop out: a person's emotional response to a new situation subsides, noises go unnoticed, and room stimuli that are not relevant are disregarded. Such a potpourri of factors specific to each new situation affect learning how to learn that it is difficult to state general principles. We can stress, however, the importance of making an early determination of the *essential* stimuli and disregarding the irrelevant aspects of the learning situation.

By way of summary, we may say that positive and negative transfer are the results of carrying over both specific components and general modes of attack from one task to another. In talking about specific components as the basis of transfer, we generally analyze an old and a current task into their respective stimulus and response components. If stimuli are varied and the response common to both tasks is kept constant, then positive transfer results. The degree of similarity between stimuli in two tasks determines the amount of positive transfer. If stimuli are kept constant and responses varied, negative transfer results in most cases. Positive transfer occurs only to the extent that the second response is compatible with and resembles the first response. Learning-to-learn phenomena are very widespread in everyday life and seem to provide the mechanism whereby subjects are able to perform with little or no error in new situations.

Remembering and Forgetting

chapter seven

For over a year psychologist Harold E. Burtt spiced his infant son's daily reading diet of *Mother Goose* and *Winnie-the-Pooh* with passages from Sophocles. Starting when the boy was fifteen months old, Burtt read three passages of twenty lines apiece daily, switching to a new set of three passages every three months until the boy was three years old and had been read twenty-one different passages. What was particularly remarkable was that Burtt read these passages to his son in the original Greek! (Burtt gives no indication of whether his son liked this regimen or not.) Five years later Burtt tested for possible vestiges of these passages in the child's memory: without explanation, he asked his son (now eight years old) to memorize some of the same passages as well as a number of other equally difficult Greek passages that the boy had neither seen nor heard before. Burtt reasoned that if the boy learned the old passages faster than the new ones, this ease in later learning could be attributed to the exposure five years earlier. Indeed, Burtt found that it took 435 repetitions for his son to learn the new passages, but only 317 to learn the old ones.

This case demonstrates rather strikingly how persistent is memory: even though the original material was classical Greek, a language that had no meaning to the little boy whatsoever, there was still an obvious retention of some kind from the original exposure.

In this chapter we shall be concerned with describing those factors which influence our ability to retain material we have learned. It is clear that understanding memory is central to understanding learning. Obviously, there could be no improvement from trial to trial if a learner did not remember something from preceding trials. We build on what we remember from previous experience. The hypothetical residue left by previous experience is often called a *habit*, or a *bond*, or more directly, a *memory trace*.

Measuring Memory

There are three basic methods psychologists use to measure memory in the laboratory: (*a*) recall; (*b*) recognition; and (*c*) relearning.

RECALL

Recall is a method that is familiar to all students who have had to write an essay examination, which is one example of a recall test. Recall requires a person to tell what he has learned by producing the correct responses. A person who can produce the lines "Four score and seven years ago our fathers brought forth on this continent a new nation . . ." shows that he knows at least a part of the Gettysburg Address. A person who tells you that Sacramento is the capital of California shows that he knows at least one state capital.

Recall is easily tested in the laboratory. In one type of experiment, called a *free-recall experiment*, subjects are presented with a list of items to examine and after some time passes are asked to recall as many items as possible. For example, subjects might be presented with a list of words (such as *flabby, police, overt, blatant, letter*, etc.) or a list of nonsense syllables (such as *bif, sed, pij, meq*, etc.). Subjects are then told to speak or write down as many items as they can, in any order that they wish. The *recall score* is the percentage correct.

RECOGNITION

Recognition is a matter of discriminating that which one has seen or learned from that which one has not seen or learned. It is what we do when we take a multiple-choice exam—when we recognize or identify choice A as being the correct one. Recognition is what we do when we see someone who looks very familiar but whose name we cannot quite remember.

In a typical recognition experiment, the subject's ability to recognize items he has just studied is tested by showing him the study items together with new ("distractor") items and asking the subject to identify the study items. Roger Shepard has done several experiments to determine how well subjects could recognize stimuli that they have seen before. In one experiment 540 words on cards were presented to the subject, who went through the deck of cards at his own speed. Next he was tested with sixty pairs of words. One word in each test pair had appeared in the deck of cards just examined, while the other word in each pair was a *distractor* (a new word); the subject's task was to pick out the card word in each instance. Subjects in this experiment recognized a remarkable number of words, on the average scoring 90 percent correct. In a similar experiment Shepard showed 612 pictures to each subject using a filmstrip projector which advanced at the subject's own pace; then subjects were shown sixty-eight pairs of pictures and asked to indicate the picture they had seen before. Subjects recognized pictures even better than words; on the average their recognition was 98.5 percent correct.

RELEARNING

Relearning is a measure of retention not commonly utilized in classroom situations. To measure the efficiency of relearning, a subject is first asked to learn something new—say, a list of nonsense syllables. After a rest period—from a few seconds to a few years—he is asked to relearn this material. Decreases in the time required, number of errors made, or trials needed to relearn the list then give us some indication of the persistence of memory. Relearning is a sensitive measure and will sometimes show the effect of memory even in cases where the other two measures do not show any effect at all—as when Burtt's son *relearned* the Greek passages that had been read to him years earlier in fewer repetitions than it took to learn similar new material. The effect of his earlier experience could only be detected by the relearning procedure; if asked to recall or even recognize the earlier passages, the boy almost certainly would have been unable to do so.

Figure 7–1 shows the variation in sensitivity, over an extended time period, of the three methods of measuring memory. Recall, inevitably, produces the lowest scores. Although the chart in Figure 7–1 indicates that recognition yields the highest retention scores, this line could easily be lowered by presenting the items to be recognized in the context of highly similar material. A nonsense syllable is easier to recognize in a group of colors than among similar syllables. This does not mean that a

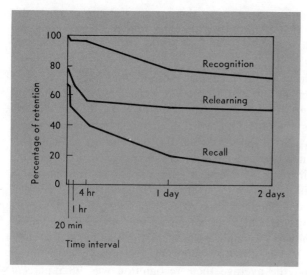

FIGURE 7–1. Amount of learning retained as a function of the method of measurement. [Adapted and simplified from C. W. Luh, *Psychol. Monogr.* 31 (1922).

memory trace is stronger when we test through relearning or recognition; it is just easier to detect when we use a more sensitive measure.

Forgetting: Five Explanations

We have sometimes referred to memory as a "trace." Psychologists are not yet in a position to state what the nature of this trace is, nor how to describe it theoretically. Nevertheless, it seems reasonable to hypothesize that events must somehow be recorded if we are to explain later recall—and if we are to explain the phenomenon of *forgetting*. Some psychologists have ascribed forgetting to the gradual *decay* of this hypothetical trace through disuse. Other psychologists have ascribed forgetting to a *changing trace*, or to *interference effects*, or to a *failure of the retrieval mechanism*; still others have claimed that forgetting is *motivated*. No one explanation accounts for all the facts that we have about forgetting; rather, each explanation accounts for some of the facts.

DECAY THEORY

The simplest view of forgetting held by some psychologists is that the mere passage of time causes memory traces to fade. We all have a wealth of experience with the rapid fading of newly learned material. We've just been introduced to a person at a party and we immediately forget his name. We've just looked up a telephone number in the phonebook and we forget it the moment we finish dialing. The plot of a book we've read or a story we've heard becomes less vivid and less complete as time passes. All of these experiences support the idea that learned material decays with the passage of time.

There is some evidence in the psychological literature to support this theory, although much more does not. How could a decay theory explain why people *do not* forget how to swim even though they may not have practiced swimming for many years? How would the theory explain why a college student may remember the Gettysburg Address learned in the sixth grade, and yet forget a much simpler piece of prose that he learned last year?—i.e., why does decay work on last year's prose and not on the Gettysburg Address? The main point here is that although the passage of time may cause some changes which lead to forgetting, time alone does not account for all that we know about forgetting. Time all by itself can no more cause forgetting than it causes the erosion of a wooden building.

TRACE-CHANGE THEORY

The trace-change theory of forgetting grows from previous perception research, which has provided evidence that one's memory of what he has seen tends to change in specific ways. For example, if a subject is shown any of the original figures in Figure 7–2, his memory of them will shift to the more symmetrical and less imperfect figures shown in the column on the far right. Each change is brought about by a different principle: *closure* (the tendency to close an open figure), *good figure* (the tendency to perfect a figure), and *symmetry* (the tendency to balance a figure). These three principles are seen as physiological processes that are built-in aspects of the functioning of brain tissue. According to this view, because of these processes the trace laid down by experience becomes a more perfect and better-balanced figure, thereby losing some of its individuating qualities. This change in the trace, then, causes us to forget the original figure. If a trace is particularly asymmetrical the eventual formation may have little relation to the original material, and considerable forgetting may be a direct result.

The earliest experiment on the trace-change hypothesis dealt with memory of perceptual form. Subjects examined an asymmetrical form such as the one at the left in Figure 7–3 and were then asked to reproduce the form repeatedly from memory. After each reproduction, the experimenter would examine the newly drawn figure for changes. The

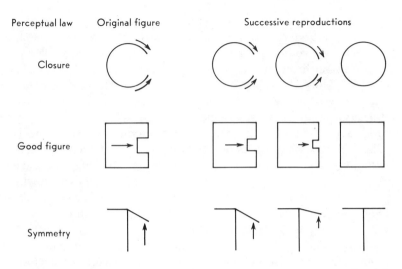

FIGURE 7–2. Progressive changes in memory traces predicted by the perceptual laws. Direction of predicted change is indicated in each case by an arrow. [From C. E. Osgood, *Method and theory in experimental psychology* (New York: Oxford University Press, 1953).]

series of drawings in Figure 7–3 shows a progressive trend toward a more symmetrical figure. In this case memory for perceptual form would seem to be changing in the direction predicted by the law of symmetry.

There is unfortunately one serious flaw in these experiments: because the same subject drew all figures for a given series, it may have been the memory trace of his own poorly drawn initial reproduction, or of his second, or third—rather than his memory trace of the original—that changed in the direction of symmetry. Yet, if the initial reproduction showed the predicted changes, is this really a valid criticism? Yes, because most of the figures used in these experiments did not have a single predictable direction of change. Therefore, it was difficult to evaluate changes that occurred. Experimenters who were favorable to the trace-change theory saw every alteration as evidence for a specific principle of

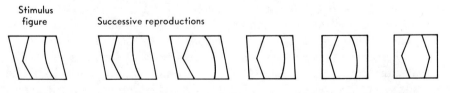

FIGURE 7–3. Successive changes in the reproduction of a single stimulus figure by the same individual. [Adapted from F. T. Perkins, *Amer. J. Psychol.* 44 (1935): 473.]

change. Similarly, experimenters who were unsympathetic to this viewpoint saw every change as fortuitous, and not dependent on any specific principles. Thus, the interpretation of the experiment finally boiled down to a question of theoretical persuasion rather than experimental fact.

To correct this error, Donald O. Hebb and E. N. Foord used figures with clearly predictable patterns of change. Two different groups of subjects were shown a stimulus figure and then tested, one group after five minutes, the other after twenty-four hours. They did *not* have to draw a reproduction of this figure; rather, *recognition* was tested by showing the subjects a series of forms, all of which differed systematically from the initial stimulus form. Figure 7–4 shows one such series.

Mistakes in recognition could veer in one of two directions: (*a*) toward the "best," most symmetrical form (the circle numbered 1), or (*b*) away from the "best" form (and toward circle 24). If the trace-change hypothesis were correct, then errors should have tended toward circle 1 (principle of closure) rather than toward circle 24. Furthermore, there should have been more such errors after twenty-four hours (during which the principle of change would have more time to be effective) than after five minutes. The results failed to reveal any such trend. Mistakes were not consistently in the direction of circle 1, nor were there more mistakes in this direction for the twenty-four-hour group than for the five-minute group. Under careful experimental conditions, then, it seems that memory traces do not change in the direction predicted by perceptual laws of change.

Does this experiment rule out the possibility that *systematic* changes in memory occur? Certainly not. In a series of ingenious experiments in which subjects reproduced stories and visual forms, F. C. Bartlett found that changes in memory are largely influenced by naming or labeling the

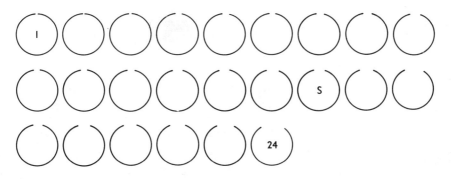

FIGURE 7–4.   Series of stimuli used to test for memory-trace change. Subjects were originally shown the stimulus labeled S. [Adapted from D. O. Hebb and E. N. Foord, *J. Exp. Psychol.* 35 (1945): 344.]

item to be memorized. The general outline of the original material does not change as much as do details relevant to the labels the subject may give to a figure. If a subject sees an ambiguous figure as resembling some object familiar to him, his reproductions will gradually alter the original until it becomes the familiar object. The label he initially gives to the ambiguous figure shapes his reproductions and his "memory trace" of the figure. More direct evidence of the role of labeling comes from an experiment done by Leonard Carmichael, H. P. Hogan, and A. A. Walters, in which subjects were first shown a group of ambiguous figures and then instructed to draw them all from memory. With one group of subjects, just before the experimenter presented each figure he told them that it looked like a particular familiar object; to the remaining subjects he remarked that the same figures looked like another familiar object. The middle column of Figure 7–5 shows materials used in this experiment. The outer columns show the types of figures reproduced along with the names of the ambiguous figures given to the two groups of subjects.

Many of the drawings show a strong effect of the naming of the mem-

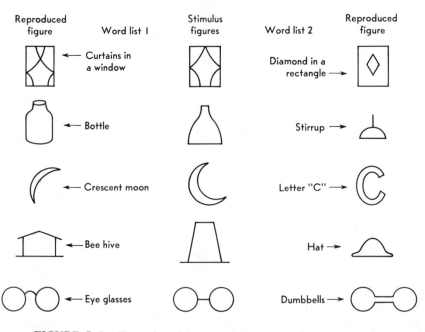

FIGURE 7–5. Examples of how a verbal label affects the reproduction of an ambiguous figure. Subjects in one group were told that the first stimulus figure looked like "curtains in a window," while subjects in the second group were told it "looked like a diamond in a rectangle." Note the differences that appear in the typical figure reproduced by the members of each group. [Adapted from L. Carmichael *et al., J. Exp. Psychol.* 15 (1932): 80.]

ory traces. Changes do occur in the reproduction of visual forms from memory, but these changes, contrary to the trace hypothesis, are largely the result of the name a subject provides for the original stimulus. In the case of the form ↑ , shown back in Figure 7–2, the reason it may be reproduced as T is that the subject has remembered it as "looking like a capital letter T." Our memory does seem to move toward symmetrical forms. Still, this may not be a result of some innate neurophysiological process. Many familiar things that have names happen also to be symmetrical.

INTERFERENCE THEORY

One of the oldest and most widely held explanations of forgetting is that people forget because of the tendency of habits to interfere with one another. How does this work? For example, suppose that in an experiment on verbal learning a subject learns the paired associate *table-weg*. After a week he returns for memory testing. During the week he has seen many tables and made many overt and covert verbal responses to the concept "table." According to interference theory, these competing responses crowd out the nonsense syllable *weg* and cause the subject to tend to forget it. On the other hand, if the subject could have avoided such postexperimental interfering experiences, a large share of this forgetting could have been prevented.

Probably the most famous study of interference was reported by J. G. Jenkins and Karl M. Dallenbach in 1924. They had two students learn a number of lists of nonsense syllables. One of the students went to sleep immediately after learning; the other student carried on with his normal daytime activities. At the end of one, two, four, and eight hours, the students were asked to recall the material they had learned. (In the case of the sleeping subject, he was awakened after each of these intervals on four different nights.) Table 3, which shows the average percentage of syllables *forgotten* after each of the four different time intervals, indicates that the sleeping subject forgot less than the awake subject in each in-

Table 3

Percentage of Syllables Forgotten
as a Function of Time and Consciousness

SUBJECT'S CONDITION	TIME ELAPSED			
	1 hr.	*2 hrs.*	*4 hrs.*	*8 hrs.*
Awake	54	69	78	91
Asleep	30	46	45	44

stance. Also worth noting is the fact that the sleeping subject forgot no more after four or eight hours' sleep than after two—probably because the bulk of his forgetting occurred during the time he lay awake before falling asleep. That he forgot 46 percent of the material during the first two hours may be explainable in terms of the time he lay awake before falling asleep or to thoughts or dreams during sleep. From the second to the eighth hour there was no significant increase in forgetting for the sleeper.

The awake subject, on the other hand, showed a progressive increase in forgetting—presumably as a consequence of performing regular daytime activities. As Jenkins and Dallenbach concluded: "Forgetting is not so much a matter of decay (due to disuse) as it is a matter of interference, inhibition or obliteration of the old by the new."

The interference theory of forgetting really consists of two subtheories: the theory that new learning can interfere with the ability to recall previously learned material, a phenomenon called *retroactive interference*; and the theory that earlier learning can interfere with the ability to recall new material, called *proactive interference*.

Retroactive interference. The interference analysis of forgetting suggests that material is lost to memory only when it is displaced by some other material. The mere passage of time between initial learning and recall does not cause forgetting. Some process or event must interpose itself to produce forgetting. In line with this, psychologists have devoted a good deal of time and energy to investigating the effect of various ways of filling the time interval between original learning and the recall of learning. A retroactive-transfer experiment is one technique that was devised for this purpose. Let us analyze one such experiment in terms of interference theory.

Most often, studies of retroactive interference have used the following three-stage procedure:

Stage 1:   A paired-associate task is presented to the subject. To make our discussion easier let us follow the fate of one pair, A-B.

Stage 2:   An interpolated pair, with the same stimulus term A and a new response term X, is presented to the subject for learning.

Stage 3:   The subject is now asked to relearn the original pair A-B or to recall B in the presence of A.

If we examine this procedure carefully we can see that the subject has learned the pair A-B in stage 1. In stage 2 he must now respond with X. When this learning is complete the subject has learned the pair A-X. Stimulus A now tends to produce both B and X; thus $A{<}^{B}_{X}$. Response X then interferes with response B in stage 3 when the A-B pair must be relearned. Forgetting of B may take place because response X is interfering.

Using a similar analysis, Arthur W. Melton and J. McQ. Irwin had five groups of subjects learn a list of nonsense syllables. This was *original learning* (stage 1). One of these groups then rested before being asked to recall the original list. The other four groups were asked to learn an interpolated list for five, ten, twenty, and forty trials, respectively. This second learning constituted *interpolated learning* (stage 2). At the end of interpolated learning all five groups were asked to recall the initial list (stage 3).

As might be predicted from interference theory, the groups that learned interpolated lists tended to have more difficulty recalling the original list. In general, the more the interpolated practice, the greater the interference.

Proactive interference. The above experiment makes it clear that one source of forgetting consists of the experiences we have between the time we learn something and the time we try to remember it. But isn't there another possible source of interference in memory? What of all the experiences that precede what we have called original learning? These produce *proactive interference*, the apparent effects of which have led many psychologists to maintain that the chief cause of forgetting in adults is old habits.

The way one psychologist tracked down the pervasive effects of proactive interference on memory reads like a piece of master detective work. Benton J. Underwood noticed that in some laboratories experimental subjects could recall as much as 80 percent of the material they had learned, whereas in other laboratories subjects were only able to recall about 10 percent. Ebbinghaus, who certainly was a master at recalling nonsense syllables, evidenced recall of only about 35 percent of the material he had learned. Could it be that a college student who had learned only one list could remember nonsense syllables better than Ebbinghaus, who had learned literally hundreds of different lists? It seemed incredible. Underwood began his investigation by examining a number of preliminary questions:

1. Were there differences in the materials used in the laboratories? By and large the answer was no.

2. Did procedures vary from laboratory to laboratory? Again the answer was generally no.

3. Did the subjects vary? Actually, the subjects did vary in terms of the amount of experience they had had in verbal-learning experiments.

Underwood sensed that this last item was the chief clue. Accordingly, he returned to all the published experiments and carefully compared the treatment of experimental subjects. After extensive sorting of evidence Underwood discovered the key to the puzzle: students in one experiment, who had learned sixteen different lists before being asked to recall the last list, recalled only about 20 percent of the material in this last list. By contrast, in a study in Underwood's laboratory where each subject learned and was asked to recall only one list, the recall rate was as high as 75 percent. After examining the reports of results in fourteen different experiments, Underwood concluded that the percentage of material that subjects can recall is clearly related to the number of previous lists they had learned (see Figure 7–6).

What this means is that interference in recall is dependent in large measure on a subject's past activities and habits before a present task. Proactive interference, in the form of already-existing habits, is probably the major cause of forgetting. The phenomenal ability of children to recall details of events long forgotten by their parents may be due to their shorter lives and consequent lesser degree of proactive interference. On the day when children begin to lose that fantastic ability to recall such details, we know they are beginning to grow up.

FORGETTING AS RETRIEVAL FAILURE

Everyone has experienced occasions when some piece of information was unavailable for recall and later, when conditions were different, it

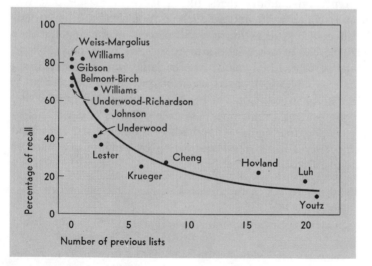

FIGURE 7–6. The effects of proactive interference on recall. Each dot represents the data obtained by a different investigator. [From B. J. Underwood, *Psychol. Rev.* 64 (1957): 53.]

came back more or less spontaneously. Because forgetting is very often a temporary rather than a permanent phenomenon, some psychologists have claimed that forgetting is not like losing something, but rather is more like being unable to find it. Forgetting occurs because of a failure in the mechanisms responsible for remembering. Often these mechanisms fail because the necessary cues for their success have not been provided.

One piece of evidence for this point of view comes from an experiment conducted by Endel Tulving and Zena Pearlstone. Typically, an experimental subject who is shown a long list of familiar words and then asked to recall the words can recall some but not all of them. In the Tulving-Pearlstone experiment, subjects were read and asked to memorize certain words in a list consisting of category names (such as *animal, weapons, crime*) and, following each category name, one or more instances of that category (e.g., *cow, bomb, treason*, for the categories just mentioned). The subjects were told just to memorize the examples following the categories, not the names of the categories themselves.

In the recall test, subjects wrote as many words as they could remember on a sheet of paper. For half the subjects the answer sheet was blank; for the other half the sheet contained all the category names. As can be seen in Figure 7–7, subjects who were provided with category names as cues recalled more words than subjects who did not.

Thus, when subjects were read a list containing twelve categories of four words each, those who were given the category names recalled about thirty words; subjects who were not given the category names recalled an average of only twenty words. Later, when this second group was also given the category cues, they were able to recall an average of twenty-eight words from the list. This means that the eight extra items that could not be recalled initially must have been stored in memory somewhere, but could not be found without additional help in the form of a retrieval cue. The results of experiments such as this one have led Tulving and Pearlstone and other psychologists to conclude that much material that appears to have been forgotten really is available in memory, but is momentarily inaccessible. Providing the proper retrieval cue, therefore, greatly facilitates recall.

MOTIVATED FORGETTING

Memories that would cause unhappiness, pain, or suffering if brought to mind are often forgotten. Most of us have but the haziest recollections of painful insults, threats to our lives, highway collisions, and other such experiences. Observations such as these have led some psychologists to conclude that much forgetting can be attributed to motivational determinants. No matter which theory of forgetting we adhere to, we

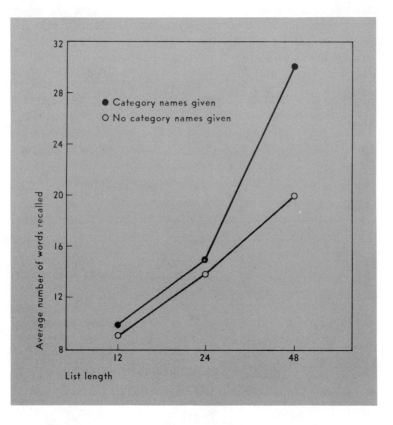

FIGURE 7–7. Mean number of category examples recalled as a function of list length for lists with four items per category. [After Tulving and Pearlstone, *J. Exp. Psychol.* (1966): 381.]

cannot ignore the motives people have for remembering and forgetting.

Forgetting through *repression* is one of the most widely discussed motivational influences on memory. Repression is the phenomenon that prevents an individual from recalling information that would cause him unhappiness. How do we know when information has been repressed? Special techniques used by psychotherapists, such as free association and hypnosis, can be used to bring repressed material to the surface and allow a person to recall things he could not recall before. Sometimes repressed content is inferred from a person's dreams or from a certain strangeness in his behavior. By use of these techniques, rather convincing evidence of the existence of repressed memories has been found.

That the techniques used to uncover repressed materials have been developed by psychotherapists does not mean that repression operates only in neurotics and similarly disturbed persons; it operates in normal people as well. In *The Psychopathology of Everyday Life*, Sigmund Freud described the effects of repression in such everyday behaviors as lapses of memory and slips of the tongue. Slips of the tongue, for example, often reveal that the speaker really believes the opposite of what he apparently intended to say, as in "He finally got smart and entrusted his money to a savings crank"; or, as a well-known psychiatrist is known to have said to a patient: "There is no use listening to your friends who know nothing about your mental condition; you are quite *incompetent* to take care of your own affairs," when, according to the therapist, he meant to say "you are quite *competent*. . . ." Freud would claim that such "speech blunders" reflect a repression of real feelings.

SUMMARY OF THEORIES OF FORGETTING

We have examined five different explanations of forgetting, each of which highlights something important. *Decay* theory claims that the passage of time is important. *Trace-change* theory claims that people systematically distort material and that these distortions produce forgetting. *Interference* theory focuses on what happens in the time interval between the learning of new material and its eventual recall. Proponents of *failure-of-retrieval* notions emphasize the importance of proper retrieval cues, while others give most of their attention to a person's *motives* in remembering and forgetting. The important thing to be learned from this section is that all these factors have to be taken into account and that all are genuine influences upon forgetting.

Short-Term and Long-Term Memory

SHORT-TERM MEMORY EXPERIMENTS

Up to this point we have discussed memory and forgetting only in terms of relatively long time intervals. But often we need to recall material immediately or very shortly after being exposed to it, and here *short-term memory* comes into play. Remembering a new telephone number, or the names of the last few streets we have passed in an unfamiliar town, or the preceding parts of this long sentence are all examples of short-term memory.

Early experiments concerning short-term memory concentrated on the memory span—the capacity of immediate memory. In a typical procedure, a subject was read progressively longer sequences of numbers or letters and then asked to recall them. The average length of the longest series he could immediately recall over a series of trials was then taken to indicate the size of his memory span.

Is memory span about the same size for all kinds of material? According to George A. Miller, the length of the average human memory span can be expressed as 7 ± 2 (read "seven plus or minus two"), meaning that an adult can normally immediately recall seven items, but may often be able to remember as many as eight or nine items or only as few as five or six. These items can be numbers, letters, nonsense syllables, or words; regardless of the material, our short-term memory capacity remains about the same. This seems rather strange when we consider that, whereas we can recall only 7 ± 2 letters, we can recall 7 ± 2 words even though the words probably have an average of five letters apiece, making a total of thirty-five letters in all. To give an example, the series *horse, crate, radio, dress, roast* is no harder to remember than the series *g-h-r-z-p*.

What we seem to recall are not the specific letters or numbers but meaningful units—"chunks" of information rather than the components of each chunk. The word *triphenylmethane* may exceed our memory span if we consider it as a series of sixteen letters. But even if we are completely unfamiliar with chemical terminology, *triphenylmethane* is easily memorized even as five "nonsense syllables."

Lloyd R. and Margaret Jean Peterson (1959) have developed a way of studying short-term memory that has yielded extremely surprising results. You would think that when shown a single three-consonant cluster ("trigram") such as *bqr*, an average college student would be capable of recalling it after eighteen seconds. As a matter of fact, most students cannot! The Petersons presented students with such a trigram and then asked for recall after retention intervals ranging from three to eighteen seconds. Each student was tested eight times at each of the recall intervals 3, 6, 9, 12, 15, and 18 seconds. Since they wanted to minimize the possibility that students would rehearse the syllable, the Petersons asked them to fill the time between presentation and testing by counting backward by threes or fours from, say, 366. Retention was found to decrease very rapidly as a function of the retention interval, declining to less than 10 percent after eighteen seconds. In other words, not more than 10 percent of the students could recall *bqr* after eighteen seconds had elapsed (see Figure 7–8).

In a similar experiment, Bennett B. Murdock, Jr., tested the ability to recall three different types of materials—nonsense syllables, common words, and sets of three unrelated words—subject to the same precaution against rehearsing used by the Petersons: that is, after the subject was presented the information he had to occupy himself with a backward-counting exercise until the time he was tested. The results for the trigrams

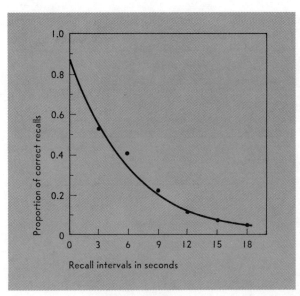

FIGURE 7–8. Short-term recall of three-letter nonsense syllables, using the Peterson and Peterson counting technique. This graph shows the proportion of correct recalls occurring with latencies of less than 2.8 seconds. Data points are actual; the curve has been fitted to these points. [From L. R. Peterson and M. J. Peterson, *J. Exp. Psychol.* (1959): 195.]

were similar to those reported by the Petersons. With the single words, however, there was little or no forgetting over the entire eighteen-second recall interval. For the sets of three unrelated words the subject's failure to recall was comparable to that found for the nonsense syllables. Murdock's complete results are shown in Figure 7–9. Notice the similarity between the curves for nonsense syllables and three-word sets in Figure 7–9 and the Petersons' curve for nonsense syllables in Figure 7–8. This similarity again suggests that the span of short-term memory is determined by the number of chunks of information to be recalled, rather than by the number of elements within an item.

THE DISTINCTION BETWEEN SHORT-TERM
AND LONG-TERM MEMORY

One of the main issues in a general theory of memory is whether the same mechanism is involved in remembering recently presented events (short-term memory, STM) as in remembering information over relatively long time intervals (long-term memory, LTM). We have all had the experience of looking up a telephone number in the telephone book

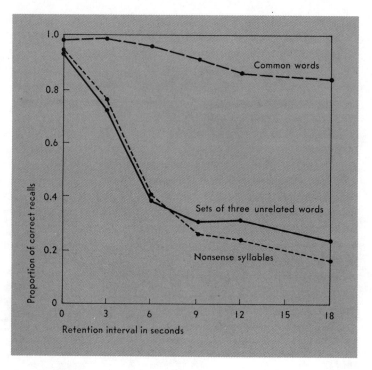

FIGURE 7–9. Comparison of recall of three-letter nonsense syllables, common words, and sets of three words. [From B. B. Murdock, *J. Exp. Psychol.* 62 (1961): 619.]

and holding it in memory just long enough to make the call. Is this process different from retaining the phone number of a friend?

Some psychologists feel that the process is the same, that the same type of storage and retrieval mechanisms are involved in both kinds of remembering. The reason usually given for this belief is that there are some experimental data on STM which can be interpreted in terms of interference factors known to operate in LTM. G. Keppel and B. Underwood, for example, have provided evidence that the main factor causing forgetting in a Peterson-Peterson task is proactive interference. Figure 7–10, which presents some of Keppel and Underwood's results, indicates that if a three-consonant item is the first item to be tested, it is remembered almost perfectly, even after an eighteen-second delay; but if the same item occurs later in the series, it is less likely to be remembered. Hence, forgetting over short intervals can be attributed to proactive inhibition resulting from previously presented items. Also, the amount of proactive inhibition increases with the length of the retention interval (between three and eighteen seconds) and this result is in agreement

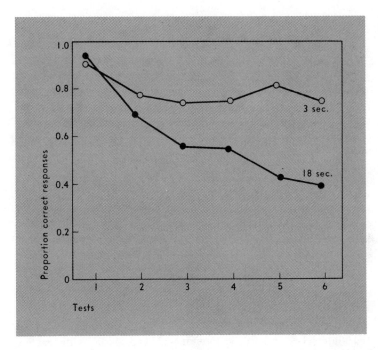

FIGURE 7–10. Retention as a function of number of prior items, and length of retention interval. [After Keppel and Underwood, *J. Verb. Learning and Verb. Behav.* (1962): 153.]

with findings regarding long-term memory. This result suggests that the same principles of interference may apply to short-term retention of items as to long-term retention of lists. Why then, should we distinguish between short- and long-term memory at all?

Psychologists who believe in two separate mechanisms—one for STM and another for LTM—use both behavioral and neurological evidence to support their position. Brenda Milner has uncovered physiological evidence in her studies of brain-damaged patients with memory deficits. Most of the patients' memory troubles occurred when they had to learn new material. Long-term memory was not affected nor was the ability to retain a few items in short-term memory. A case history best illustrates the difficulties these patients had when they attempted to learn something new.

[One patient] was a 29-year old motor-winder who had been rendered incapable of work by his frequent severe seizures. Because of his desperate condition, Dr. Scoville carried out radical bilateral medial temporal lobe resection on Sept. 1, 1953. I first saw him 20 months later, at which time he gave the date as March, 1953, and his age as

27. He knew that he had had a brain operation, but I think only because the possibility had been entertained for so many years before the operation was actually performed. He kept saying "It is as though I am just waking up from a dream; it seems as though it had just happened."

As far as we can tell this man has retained little if anything of events subsequent to operation, although his I.Q. rating is actually slightly higher than before. Ten months before I examined him his family had moved from their old house to one a few blocks away on the same street. He still has not learned the new address, though remembering the old one perfectly, nor can he be trusted to find his way home alone. He does not know where objects constantly in use are kept; for example, his mother still has to tell him where to find the lawn-mower, even though he may have been using it only the day before. She also states that he will do the same jigsaw puzzles day after day without showing any practice effect and that he will read the same magazines over and over again without finding their contents familiar. (Milner, 1959, p. 49.)

What is interesting about this patient, and many like him, is that he behaves normally as long as he can hold incoming information in short-term memory. He can hold it there by concentrating intensely or by repeating the material over and over again. As soon as he is distracted, the material is lost. Another patient studied by Milner said, "My brain feels like a sieve, I forget everything." The observation that short-term retention occurs and that already-established patterns of long-term retention can be used—but that there is an inability to establish new patterns of long-term retention (as in remembering a new address)—lends support to the view that a functional difference exists between long-term and short-term memory.

Because experiments by Keppel and Underwood and others have shown that interference causes forgetting in both LTM and STM, several psychologists have claimed that the distinction between the two forms of memory is not a valid one. This view can be challenged, however, on the grounds that the type of interference causing forgetting in STM is different from the type causing forgetting in LTM. Items which interfere in STM are those that sound alike; that is, if you present letters of the alphabet to a subject, he is most likely to confuse letters that sound alike. R. Conrad, for example, visually presented six letters to subjects at a rate of one every three-quarters of a second and then asked the subjects to recall them. Errors in recall typically involved letters that sounded alike; e.g., if *p* had been presented, subjects often recalled *b*. Even though the presentation was visual, the subjects' confusions were based on sound similarity, implying that the interference in STM involves acoustic confusion regardless of the original form of the material.

In LTM, however, items which interfere with one another are typically those that are similar in meaning. Thus, for LTM, semantic interference seems to be a major factor. The fact that two different types of interference affect short-term and long-term memory has been taken as grounds for contending that STM and LTM must be two different systems, operating on the basis of related, but different, memory principles.

This issue has not been resolved. A new type of experiment would seem to be needed in order to resolve this controversy; in any case, for the present it seems necessary and wise to draw the distinction between these two systems.

PROCESSES IN SHORT-TERM MEMORY

With the distinction between short-term and long-term memory somewhat in hand, let us turn to the problem of how we retrieve information from short-term memory. Before we discuss the retrieval process, it is important to make some distinctions among possible processes. Two alternatives that we shall consider here are a *successive-scanning process* and a *parallel process*. An analogy will help explain the difference between these processes. Suppose that, deciding to wear a pair of red socks one day, you go into the bedroom, open the dresser drawer containing your socks, and start looking through them one by one; you would be conducting a successive-scanning process. If, however, you open the drawer and examine the entire drawer's contents all at once, you would be conducting a parallel process. It may seem intuitively obvious to you that when you open a drawer of socks, the red ones "pop out" at you. It "feels" as if you do not search through the socks one at a time, and thus a parallel process must be involved in this search. But how do you know for sure? Perhaps you are scanning your socks one at a time at such a fast rate that it "feels" as if you are seeing them all at once. Similarly, when a person is shown the queen of hearts from a deck of cards, he can easily recognize this card and say, "It's the queen of hearts." How can he do that so quickly? Does he decide that it's a queen and then decide that it's a heart (a successive-scanning process)? Or does he decide first that it is a heart (another successive-scanning process)? Or does he decide on both dimensions at once (a parallel process)? As yet this specific question has not been answered, but the illustration should help clarify the difference between a successive-scanning and a parallel process.

Let us now return to the issue of short-term-memory retrieval. One question that arises is whether the retrieval process involves successive scanning or not. A well-known psychologist at Bell Laboratories, Saul Sternberg, has provided an answer to this question. In Sternberg's experiments, a subject is shown a *memory set*, which usually consists of a set of from one to six digits. For example, the subject might be asked to memorize the set 2, 5, 3, 1. Soon afterward, a *target* digit is shown to the subject and he must decide whether the target was a member of the memory set. The subject presses one of two buttons to answer "yes" or "no," as quickly as he can, and his reaction time (RT) is measured from the moment the target appears until he responds. Sternberg was specifically interested in the relationship between reaction time and the size of the memory set. Figure 7–11 depicts this relationship as Sternberg observed it in his actual data. Notice that there is a positive relationship between RT and memory-set size: the larger the memory set, the longer the RT. Also, the data charted in Figure 7–11 reveal that RT is about 38 milliseconds (38 thousandths of a second) longer for sets with two digits than for sets with one digit, and 38 milliseconds longer for sets with three digits than for sets with two digits. In other words, for each additional member of the memory set, RT is approximately 38 milliseconds longer.

Sternberg's results suggest that in the process of short-term-memory retrieval a successive-scanning process takes place—that is, the person compares the target digit successively to each member of the memory set, each of these comparisons taking roughly the same amount of time (38 milliseconds).

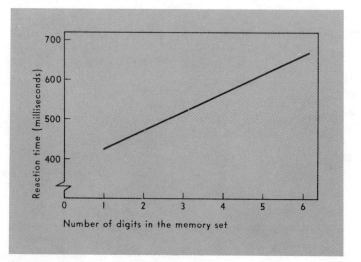

FIGURE 7–11. Reaction time to answer "yes" or "no" to a target digit as a function of the number of digits in the memory set. [Adapted from S. Sternberg, High-speed scanning in human memory, *Science* (August 5, 1966):153, 652–54, Fig. 5. © 1966 by the American Association for the Advancement of Science.]

PROCESSES IN LONG-TERM MEMORY

Long-term memory contains a great deal of information. It contains facts about our personal experiences, such as the events of the day we graduated high school or what we did last weekend. It also contains another kind of information called "semantic" information. In a recent paper by Endel Tulving, the phrase *semantic memory* was used to refer to the organized knowledge we possess about words and other verbal symbols, their meaning, and referents; about relationships among them; and about rules, formulas, and algorithms for manipulating them. These millions of items are part of our long-term memories, and there is no doubt that we are very good at reaching into that store and producing the exact response appropriate to many questions asked of us. We're very good at reaching in and producing the answer to a question that we have been asked before, such as "Who was the first president of the United States?" But we're just as good at producing a particular response to questions which we've never before been asked in a particular way. For example, if someone asks for the name of an animal beginning with the letter z, or the name of a large country, we don't have much trouble. But how do we do it? By what process are we able to answer with a response that is uniquely appropriate to the question?

J. Freedman and E. Loftus posed the question more specifically: If a person is required to search through long-term memory to retrieve instances of a category, does this retrieval involve some kind of successive-scanning process? Freedman and Loftus required subjects to produce an instance of a member of a category, subject to some restrictions—e.g., "Name a fruit beginning with p"—and measured the time subjects needed to do this. They reasoned that if retrieval involves a successive search through the category—i.e., if subjects perform such a task by going through instances of fruits until they find one beginning with p—then it should take longer to name a member of a larger category than that of a smaller one. That is, for example, it should take longer to find a fruit starting with p than a season starting with w. This result turned out not to be true—i.e., it took no longer to name a member of a large category than that of a small one. Freedman and Loftus thus concluded that whatever long-term memory retrieval consists of, it does not consist of a successive-scanning process.

One of the major problems in studying retrieval from long-term memory is that we do not know exactly how the material stored in memory was learned in the first place, nor do we know its precise organization or structure. In order to postulate a retrieval mechanism, we need a structure to retrieve from. To use an analogy, how can we retrieve a book from a large library unless we know how the books are organized or structured or arranged in the library? Structure is a major factor determining retrieval. To get around this problem many psychologists have postulated both a structure and a retrieval mechanism. If an experiment supports the proposed theory, it supports both the structure and the retrieval mechanism. If, on the other hand, an experiment does not support the theory, there is no way to know whether it is the structure or the theory that is wrong.

What kind of structure has been postulated? Freedman and Loftus, following the lead of Allan Collins and Ross Quillian, have suggested that the structure of long-term memory is hierarchical in nature. Figure 7–12 depicts a portion of a hypothetical memory structure proposed by Collins and Quillian. Information about *animals* is divided into information about *birds* and *fish*. Information about *birds* is further subdivided into information about specific birds, such as *canaries* and *bluebirds*. An important assumption about this network is that a property which characterizes a particular class of things is stored only at the place in the hierarchy that corresponds to that class. For example, a property that characterizes all animals such as the fact that they eat or drink is stored only at "*animal*." It is not stored again with the different varieties of animals, even though they also eat and drink. Similarly, with *birds* is stored the property "*flies*," which is relevant to most birds. This information is

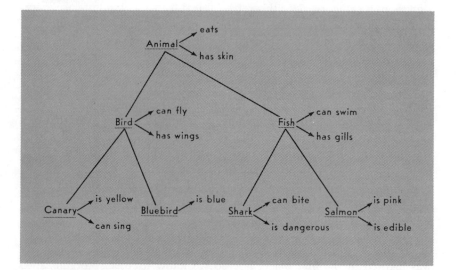

FIGURE 7–12. Part of a hierarchically organized memory structure. [After Collins and Quillian, *J. Verb. Learning and Verb. Behav.* 8 (1969): 240.]

not stored again with *canary, bluebird,* or other specific birds. And, with *canary* is stored information that is relevant to all canaries, such as the fact that they are yellow. This is the structure proposed by Collins and Quillian. Now let's turn to retrieval. Suppose we ask a person to answer various questions about canaries. Which questions do you think would take longer to answer than others?

1. Does a canary eat?
2. Does a canary fly?
3. Is a canary yellow?

If you guessed that question 3 would be more quickly answered than question 2, and question 2 more quickly than 1, you would be correct. The actual data are shown in Figure 7–13. Collins and Quillian explain that to answer question 3 you first have to enter the level in memory corresponding to "*canary,*" where you would immediately find the information that canaries are yellow and thus be able to answer this question relatively quickly. In the case of question 2, you would not find any information at that level of memory concerning whether canaries fly. However, since a canary is a bird, you would move up the hierarchy to the level where "*birds*" is stored and would then find that birds fly, and

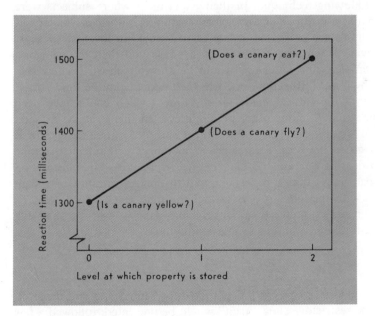

FIGURE 7–13. Reaction time taken to answer various questions about nouns and their properties. [After Collins and Quillian, 1969.]

so you would conclude that a canary must fly. Question 2 thus takes a little longer to answer than question 3. The reason question 1 takes the longest time to answer is that you do not find information about whether canaries eat stored either at the level of "*canary*" or at the level of "*birds*." You must go up an additional level in the hierarchy to decide that a canary (which is a bird and thus—because a bird is an animal) eats. The additional time thus spent moving from level to level to level in the hierarchy accounts for the longer time it takes to answer question 1 than the other two questions.

Looking more closely at Figure 7–13, notice that the average person takes about 90 milliseconds (about one-tenth of a second) longer to answer question 3 than to answer question 2, and about 90 milliseconds longer to answer question 2 than to answer question 1. What does this 90 milliseconds represent? According to Collins and Quillian, it is the time necessary to travel from one level of the hierarchy to the next.

If we estimate that it takes a little under a tenth of a second to move from one level of a semantic hierarchy to another, can we estimate how long it takes to reach the hierarchy in the first place? Collins and Quillian, and Freedman and Loftus, assume that the first step of the retrieval process is to enter the hierarchy at the appropriate place. Freedman and Loftus obtained an estimate of the time needed to enter the hierarchy using the following technique. In their experiment where subjects were asked to name a member of a category beginning with a particular letter, the stimuli were presented in one of two ways. In the first strategy, the letter was shown first, followed by a pause and then the category. So, for example, "first letter, *p*" would be shown, followed a few seconds later by "fruit." Reaction time was then taken from the time "fruit" appeared until the subject made his response (which could have been "peach" or "pear," among other possibilities). In this strategy, as soon as the word "fruit" was shown, the subject had to do three things. First, he had to go to his "*fruit*" category in memory. Let us call the time needed to do this t_1. Next he had to retrieve the relevant information from the category—that is to say, he had to find an instance of a fruit that begins with the letter *p*. Let us call the time needed to do this t_2. Finally, he had to produce a response, which takes a time we shall call *k*. Thus the total reaction time in this condition is:

$$RT_1 = t_1 + t_2 + k$$

In the second strategy, the category was presented first and then followed by the restrictor. Thus, "fruit" would be presented, followed a few seconds later by "first letter, *p*." Reaction time was then taken from "first letter, *p*" to the response. In this strategy it is possible for the subject to enter the category during the interval between "fruit" and "first letter, p." Thus the time t_1 is not included in the total RT, which in this case is:

$$RT_2 = t_2 + k$$

By subtracting RT_2 from RT_1, we can get an estimate of t_1, the time needed to go to the category. In practice t_1 turned out to be about 250 milliseconds (or a quarter of a second).

So far, then, it appears that many experiments are consistent with the notion that long-term memory is arranged hierarchically. This hypothesis, plus the two-stage retrieval scheme which we have just discussed, seems to give a fairly accurate description of the available data.

Special Topics in Memory

chapter eight

Improving Memory

Is there anyone who has not wished for a perfect memory, for the ability to remember any conversation, any lecture, any passage from a book? Thousands of people flock to courses on memory training each year searching for various tricks, gimmicks, and methods to improve their memories. But do these courses do any good? Do they really improve anyone's memory? In this chapter, we shall discuss three approaches to the problem of improving memory; one of them has not been successful, while the other two have worked quite well. The three approaches are: (*a*) strengthening the memory faculty by practice; (*b*) using mnemonic techniques; and (*c*) self-recitation.

STRENGTHENING THE MEMORY FACULTY BY PRACTICE

In 1891 William James wondered whether practice in memorization would enable him to memorize new material more easily. For eight days in a row he daily memorized 158 lines of *Satyr* by Victor Hugo. He then spent thirty-eight days memorizing the first book of *Paradise Lost* in addition to other selections of poetry and prose. Did all this practice in memorizing improve his memory? The second 158 lines from *Satyr* took *longer* to learn than the first 158 lines! After all that effort there was no improvement in his ability to memorize new material. But we must be careful of how we interpret this result. William James was an intellectually accomplished man; he was a psychologist who was interested in and had studied a great deal about learning. It is possible that at the beginning of the experiment his ability to memorize was so well developed that there was no room for further improvement. This could have been the reason why practice had no effect.

In an experiment reported in the *British Journal of Psychology*, W. G. Sleight supervised practice in memorizing by twelve-year-old girls. Some of the girls practiced memorizing poetry; others practiced memorizing scientific formulas, and others, geographical distances. The practice continued for thirty minutes a day, four days a week, for a total of six weeks. At the end of this period, the girls showed no improvement whatsoever in their ability to memorize.

If practice doesn't help, what does? Mnemonic systems are sometimes used as the basis of courses which claim to develop a "superpower memory." Do they work?

MNEMONIC TECHNIQUES

The term *mnemonics* refers to an assortment of techniques for elaborating and organizing information so that it can be more easily memorized. In addition to discovering whether mnemonics really help us remember better, another reason for examining mnemonics is to see if they can give us some valuable clues into the nature of memory itself.

Mnemonic devices have been around for a long time; the ancient Greeks used them to remember all sorts of things. There is a wonderful anecdote about the Greek poet Simonides that illustrates the type of mnemonic used by Roman teachers of rhetoric. Cicero (in *De Oratore*) claimed that during the time of Greek civilization Simonides, after reciting poetry at a banquet given by a nobleman of Thessaly, was abruptly drawn away from the banquet hall by a messenger of the gods Castor and Pollux. Moments later, the entire roof of the hall caved in. All of the other guests were crushed to death beneath the ruins, and their bodies were so mutilated that none of the victims could be identified. The relatives were desperate—how were they to bury their dead loved ones? Simonides found that he was able to remember the exact place where each person had been sitting, and thus was able to identify the bodies. On the basis of this experience, Simonides wondered if it would be possible to use this technique in remembering objects and ideas. Couldn't we, he reasoned, better recall objects and ideas by assigning them fixed positions in space? Simonides, said to be the inventor of the art of memory, showed that we can. This particular mnemonic device came to be called the "method of loci."

At one time or another, we all have used mnemonics to solve everyday problems. When we had to learn the proper ordering of the letters *i* and *e* (in English), we learned "*i* before *e*, except after *c*." When we were learning the number of days in each month, we learned "Thirty days hath September. . . ." Some of us learned the order of the planets by remembering "Men Very Easily Make All Jobs Serve Useful Needs Promptly" (Mercury, Venus, Earth, Mars, asteroids, Jupiter, Saturn, Uranus, Neptune, Pluto). Many visitors to New York City rely on the phrase "Ladies Prefer Men" to remember the order of Lexington, Park, and Madison avenues. There is no doubt that we deliberately use mnemonics of all kinds, and they do help us learn faster and recall better.

Recently, anecdotes in support of mnemonics have been supplemented by rigorous laboratory experiments. In a study done by Gordon Bower and Michal Clark, students were given a list of ten unrelated words and were told to learn them in the order they appeared on the list. Half the students were asked to learn the words by making up and weaving a story around the words; the other half were given the words and simply told to memorize them for recall. Recall of the list immediately after it was studied was perfect for both groups of students. The same procedure was then repeated with eleven additional lists of words. After all twelve lists had been studied, students were given the first word of the first list and asked to respond with the remaining words in the list. This procedure was then repeated for the remaining lists. Students who had made up stories recalled an average of 93 percent of the words; students in the other group recalled an average of only 13 percent of the words. This example shows that the use of a simple mnemonic technique increased recall by a factor of almost 7—i.e., students who made up stories recalled almost seven times as many words as the students who did not.

It appears that mnemonic techniques improve our ability to memorize by relating new material to some previously learned and already organized material. Simonides knew that the various guests at the banquet were seated in different physical locations. He recalled each guest by visualizing each location and thereby "seeing" again the guest who had occupied it. In the laboratory experiment, students who organized words into stories outperformed those students who relied on sheer rote drill. If we first organize words into a meaningful structure (e.g., a story), then recalling the story will facilitate recall of the words. Simonides realized that one of the basic principles of the art of memory depends on orderly arrangement, and it seems clear that a critical reason mnemonics work is because they organize material into such "orderly arrangements."

SELF-RECITATION

Suppose that you have two hours to read a history assignment. It takes thirty minutes to read through the whole assignment once. Should you spend the two hours reading the assignment four times? Or should you read the assignment once and then stop to ask yourself questions about it? Or should you recite the assignment to yourself, and then reread it again?

An experiment by A. Gates dramatically shows the greater effectiveness of self-recitation or quizzing yourself. The materials that his students learned consisted of both nonsense syllables and short biographies. Table 4 presents the results for nonsense syllables.

Notice that subjects performed best when they spent only 20 percent of their time reading the syllables and 80 percent of their time in self-recitation. The results for short biographies were similar. Other investigators have also shown greater recall for definitions, French vocabulary, spelling and arithmetic when self-recitation was used.

Let us briefly summarize what we have found out about improving memory. Practice alone doesn't help. We do not seem to be able to strengthen our ability to remember by memorizing lots of material. Being able to organize the material we want to remember, however, will help greatly. When parts of the material to be remembered can be woven into systematic relations with each other and with what the person has already learned, then the learning and recall of the material is strongly

Table 4

The Value of Self-Recitation in Memorizing Nonsense Syllables

PERCENTAGE OF TIME DEVOTED TO SELF-RECITATION (WITH REMAINDER TO READING)	PERCENTAGE OF SIXTEEN NONSENSE SYLLABLES RECALLED	
	Immediately	*After 4 hr*
0	35	15
20	50	26
40	54	28
60	57	37
80	74	48

facilitated. Mnemonics help us to organize in this way. In addition, self-recitation is a much more efficient way of learning material than is reading and rereading the same material—probably because the self-recitation method demands the same kind of active participation from the learner that later will be demanded of him when the book is closed.

Memory Disorders

In a recent book called *Disorders of Memory and Learning*, George Talland describes this case:

One day a practically illiterate epileptic patient stood up, while under seizure, and preached a funeral sermon in Latin. He could not possibly have heard the sermon in full before, but must have heard bits and snatches of it on several different occasions. When the seizure was over he could not remember a single word of the sermon; in fact, he never could understand Latin at all. Hypnosis was tried, but still he remembered nothing of his performance.

This is obviously an example of a memory disorder. Psychiatric literature is filled with thousands and thousands of such reports, many of them quite well documented. The study of such disorders is important both practically and theoretically. Theoretically, the study of memory disorders might provide information as to how memory processes operate when they are intact. Practically speaking, a detailed knowledge of the nature and extent of a particular person's memory defect better enables us to help him. One way we can help is by training him to use what memory abilities he does have in order to compensate for deficiencies.

There are occasions in everyone's life when he or she has had small lapses in memory, but certainly we wouldn't want to call these lapses "memory defects." We've all known other people who have witnessed the same event that we have witnessed, and yet remember it in slightly (or even grossly) different ways. We wouldn't call this a disorder. Nor do we say that a boyfriend who "forgets" to show up for a date or an "absentminded professor" who forgets where he last put his glasses are suffering from memory disorders. If they tried to remember, presumably they could. But, when someone can't remember who is really concentrating, who is really trying to retrieve some information relating to personal experiences that he could easily remember just a short while before, then we are more inclined to believe that this failure is due to a disorder of some sort.

In this section we shall discuss two types of memory disorders: *neurogenic* defects, which are attributable to brain lesions or other forms of bodily damage; and *psychogenic* defects, associated with emotional shocks and stresses or with unconscious motives and without concomitant brain damage. The section concludes with a description and discussion of "S.," a man who remembered only too well.

NEUROGENIC (ORGANIC) DISORDERS

Korsakoff's syndrome. In 1887 the Russian physician S. S. Korsakoff published a description of a patient whose problem was an inability to hold new information in memory for more than a few seconds. The patient was constantly losing things and losing his way around the hospital. On several occasions, he got lost going from his bed to the bathroom. He forgot who his last visitor was five minutes after the visitor had gone. He could not recognize his own sketches after a delay of a minute or so. He had no idea when he had entered the hospital—was it yesterday or last year? The patient had no trouble remembering events that had occurred before his illness, and he could also hold several items in short-term memory.

The symptoms should sound familiar, for they are similar to the symptoms observed by Brenda Milner and described on pages 121–122. This particular defect has variously been called "Korsakoff's syndrome," mental deficiency, or simply "the memory defect." Originally Korsakoff thought it was due to brain damage resulting from chronic alcoholism. Now, however, it is known that while alcoholism can trigger the syndrome, the disorder can also be caused by a variety of other factors. In addition, it seems likely that the defect is caused specifically by destruction of brain tissues in an area of the brain called the hippocampus.

Epilepsy. An epileptic seizure is often accompanied by hallucinations and spontaneous actions; typically, however, the patient can later recall nothing about events that occurred during the fit or events that preceded the fit by at least a few seconds. Sometimes an event that occurred hours before the seizure is "wiped" from the patient's memory. The forgetting of events that occurred prior to a seizure (or prior to any trauma or illness) is referred to as *retrograde amnesia*. Often some of the "lost" memories will later emerge spontaneously; others may be recalled on some later occasion and then "forgotten" again. Not uncommon are cases in which a patient cannot remember events which took place after his seizure.

The phenomenon of forgetting events which occurred prior to an epileptic seizure provides support for a *consolidation* theory of memory. This theory assumes that immediately after learning some new material, the memory trace needs time to consolidate or "set" if it is to become a part of long-term memory. Before the trace consolidates it is very unstable, and interfering events (such as a seizure) can easily obliterate it. If nothing interferes during the brief period after learning, then, according to the theory, the memory trace consolidates and is stored.

Traumatic amnesias. A motorcyclist was riding along a dark road late one windy night when he was knocked down by another motorcyclist. When a doctor arrived at the scene of the accident—also on a motorcycle—he found the victim unconscious. A few moments later, while the doctor was examining him, the victim recovered consciousness. The following day, the victim swore that the doctor had rammed into him and was to blame for the accident. Even when the cyclist who was truly to blame came forward and claimed responsibility, the patient persisted in his belief that the doctor was responsible.

Concussions and wounds from accidents and war cause *traumatic amnesias*. In the case of the cyclist, a head injury wiped out a brief segment of memory without disturbing memory for preceding or subsequent events. Much more typically, head-injury victims cannot remember events that occurred for a period of time before and after recovery of consciousness. Boxers, for example, have been known to keep on fighting after a concussion, having no memory of their performance at all. In terms of the consolidation theory, a blow to the head disrupts the memory trace, preventing it from becoming a permanent memory.

PSYCHOGENIC DISORDERS

We have already discussed motivated forgetting and repression and concluded that motives have an important effect on what material we forget and what we remember. In this section we shall describe a few other memory derangements that appear to be emotionally determined.

Emotional amnesia. There once was a patient named Irene, a girl in her twenties who had nursed her mother through long and agonizing years of tuberculosis. After her mother died she watched her mother's body progressively waste away as it lay in a crowded, dirty, bug-ridden attic. On many occasions the girl attempted to revive the dead body or to lift the corpse onto the bed, both unsuccessfully. The mother was buried, and soon after Irene talked of suicide. She walked in her sleep, but later had no recollection of any activity during sleep. Often during these somnambulist attacks, she uttered ear-piercing shrieks and was overwhelmed by hallucinations, many of them reliving the circumstances surrounding her mother's slow, painful death. But between these attacks Irene acted as if she had totally forgotten her mother, the illness, the dying, and all of the unpleasantness. She forgot the date of her mother's death, and the cause, and often she would admonish herself for not taking better care of her mother. And why didn't she now feel more sorrow? This is a clear example of a memory disorder that is emotionally caused, and it illustrates one obvious way in which this and similar cases of amnesia are different from normal forgetting: in normal forgetting remote events are less well remembered; in cases of amnesia, it is usually the most recent events that are the most severely affected.

What can we learn from observations of people with disturbed memory function? Such observations, aside from being interesting in and of themselves, can provide clues to the processes involved in normal memory. Investigations of memory disorders have suggested, and in many cases have provided support for, many of the specific assumptions that we hold about normal memory function. Studies of patients suffering from Korsakoff's syndrome have supported the distinction between short-term and long-term memory storage. Studies of epileptic patients lend support to the idea that long-term-memory traces undergo progressive strengthening or consolidation with the passage of time.

Thus, the theories of the experimental psychologist studying memory are often confirmed (or refuted) by clinical observations. Conversely, the methods of the experimental psychologist have helped to improve the systematic observation of psychopathological cases and to translate such observations and loosely formulated explanations into testable hypotheses which will eventually contribute to our understanding and curing of mental disorders.

A PERFECT MEMORY?

What would it be like to have no limit whatsoever on the amount of material you could remember? What if you could remember the name of every person you ever met and of every place you had ever been?

A professor of psychology at the University of Moscow, Alexander Luria, presents an account of a very exceptional individual in his book *The Mind of a Mnemonist* (1968)—"a little book about a vast memory." The man, called only S., had been a newspaper reporter and came to Luria's laboratory at the suggestion of his editor. Every morning the editor would hand out assignments to his staff which consisted of long lists of people they should see, places they should go, and things they should remember to do that day. Every member of the staff took extensive notes . . . except S. He never wrote anything down. The editor finally became angry, and approached S. to scold him for not doing a good job. To the editor's surprise, S. repeated the entire assignment word for word. Not only that, but he could repeat the previous day's assignment as well. In fact, he could tell the editor what he had done at any time. For example, "one year, 9 months and 5 days ago—it was a Tuesday—you

wanted me to speak to 3 patients and 2 doctors at the Budenko Neurological Hospital in Moscow at 4:00 p.m. However it rained that day and
so I went the next day." This type of recall was easily within S.'s capa-
bility. The editor immediately sent S. to have some experiments done on
his memory, and that is how he met Dr. Luria.

S. was 29 years old. One of the first things Luria did was to present
S. with a series of words. S. listened to them and then repeated the words
back in exactly the same order as they had been presented to him. A
normal person can remember about seven words; S. had no trouble with
seventy.

It didn't matter if Luria used lists of words, numbers, or letters;
whether he presented them slowly or quickly; whether they were presented orally or in written form—S. could always reproduce the list ac-
curately. S. could also reproduce the lists in reverse order; people with
normal memories cannot do this very easily even with lists that are overlearned. To convince yourself of this point, try saying the alphabet in
reverse order or spelling the word "trouble" backwards (without looking, of course). One last observation: S. could retain these lists indefi-
nitely—not merely for a few seconds or minutes, but for weeks, months,
and even ten to twenty years!

How did S. do it? A quotation from Luria's book relates one of his
methods:

> When S. read through a long series of words, each word would elicit
> a graphic image. And since the series was fairly long, he had to find
> some way of distributing these images in a mental row or sequence.
> Most often (and this habit persisted throughout his life), he would
> "distribute" them along some roadway or street he visualized in his
> mind. . . . Frequently he would take a mental walk along that street
> . . . and slowly make his way down, "distributing" his images at
> houses, gates, and in store windows. . . . This technique of converting
> a series of words into a series of graphic images explains why S. could
> so readily reproduce a series from start to finish or in reverse order;
> how he could rapidly name the word that preceded or followed one I'd
> selected from the series. To do this he would simply begin his walk,
> either from the beginning or end of the street, find the image of the
> object I had named, and "take a look at" whatever happened to be
> situated on either side of it.   (Luria, 1968, pp. 31–33.)

It appears as if S. discovered for himself the mnemonic method of loci
used by Simonides during early Greek civilization.

Luria was quick to discover that the consequences of having such a
spectacular memory were not all good. S. had a great deal of trouble
grasping the information in simple prose passages. Images kept rising to
the surface of his mind and S. had to struggle against them. Every word

gave rise to an image and often the image was not appropriate for the passage as a whole. S. would begin to follow an image and completely lose the gist of what he was reading. "What happens is that I just can't read, can't study, for it takes up such an enormous amount of my time," is how S. himself described the experience.

S. had considerable trouble with synonyms, homonyms, and metaphors. Most of us have no problems with theŝe; we are not confused by the fact that a small child is sometimes referred to as a "child" and sometimes as a "baby." But S. was thrown off balance when such synonyms were used interchangeably within a story, and thus making sense out of the story took vast amounts of time.

The moral of this true story may be that the vast majority of us are far better off with our "imperfect" memories than S. with his nearly perfect memory.

The Role of Imagery

In this chapter we have come across the topic of imagery in relation to memory at least twice. The first instance was in the section on mnemonic techniques, where we described the method of loci used by the Greek poet Simonides. Simonides used imagery to visualize where each person had been sitting in the huge banquet hall, and on this basis he named each of the mangled bodies. The second example of the effectiveness of imagery in remembering is provided by Luria's patient, S., who relied extensively on visual imagery to remember the masses of information that he retained for years and years.

Was there something special about Simonides and S. that allowed them to use imagery to remember better, or could anyone benefit by using visual imagery? An experiment by J. Ross and K. A. Lawrence (1968) suggests that imagery will help any normal, intelligent adult to remember better. In Ross and Lawrence's experiment, college students were presented with a list of forty nouns. The students were then instructed to conjure up a mental image of the object represented by each noun as it was read off, and then to associate each image with a particular location on campus. For example, if the first word was *banana*, a student might try to imagine a bunch of bananas hanging from the door of the school cafeteria (see Figure 8–1). Thus when the entire list had been presented and this student was asked to recall the words, he could simply make a mental tour of the campus and automatically "see" the other main objects in his images. Visualizing the cafeteria door, for example, would allow him to recognize and name "banana." When students studied their list of nouns in this way their recall scores were spec-

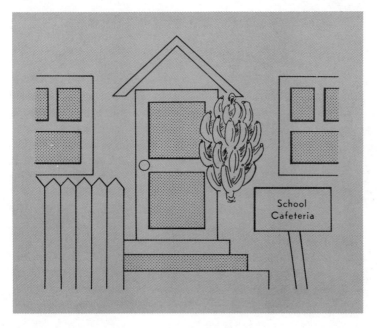

FIGURE 8–1. An example of imagery: visualizing the cafeteria door recalls the word "banana."

tacular; immediately after studying the list just once, subjects could recall an average of thirty-eight out of forty nouns in their correct serial order. This experiment provides a clear demonstration that imagery really works in aiding memory.

After such a demonstration we are left wondering exactly why imagery works so well. Some psychologists offer a verbal explanation of the effectiveness of imagery instructions in learning. They claim that when you tell a person to visualize a scene in order to link two words together, you simply encourage him to find a linguistic relationship between the two words or concepts. If, in a paired-associate experiment, the subject must remember the pair *horse-banana*, an instruction to visualize might lead him to link the two words with a phrase such as *Horse eats banana*. And, in fact, if you instruct a subject to construct such phrases, without mentioning imagery at all, his recall is almost as good as the recall of subjects who are given explicit instructions to visualize.

There is, though, considerable evidence contradicting a simple verbal explanation of imagery effects. For example, Gordon Bower told subjects to study sentences like *Horse eats banana* and *Cow kicks ball*. Some subjects were told to visualize the scene described, while others were told simply to read the sentences. The results for one experiment showed that when the subjects imagined the scene they scored 62 percent correct recall; subjects who merely read the sentences averaged 42 percent correct recall.

If the verbal view cannot explain the effects of imagery, what view can? A popular view point currently held by Gordon Bower, Allan Paivio, and other psychologists is that memory involves two components: a nonverbal, imagery process and a verbal, symbolic process. In memory experiments, when the items to be remembered are pictures or objects, it is likely that both processes are at work—i.e., both a pictorial memory trace and a verbal memory trace will be established. When the items to be remembered are words, and particularly when they are names of concrete objects like *cow*, the item *may* evoke a visual image, and possibly two memory traces will also be established here. In contrast, when the items are abstract words (like *democracy* or *clever*), they will most likely arouse no visual images, and only verbal memory traces will be established. Thus we have an explanation for the fact that objects and pictures are remembered better than concrete words, which in turn are remembered much better than abstract words.

One piece of evidence for this dual-processing trace comes from a recent experiment by Richard Freund. Freund showed subjects slides of scenic pictures taken from the home slide collections of Richard Atkinson and other friends of his at Stanford University. Subjects who had to describe or label each picture as they viewed it had much higher recognition memory than subjects who only viewed the picture and remained silent. Having to describe pictures verbally insured that a verbal as well as a pictorial memory trace was established.

The conclusion that emerges from all of this work is that mental imagery is a very effective aid to improving memory. This seems to be the case when simple paired associates are used or when more complicated (and more important) materials are used. If, however, we concentrate solely on the imagery aroused by verbal stimuli, we are likely to miss the meaning for the image. When this happens, we enter the mind of a mnemonist, and discover that perfect memory is as much a curse as it is a blessing.

Index